SMOS & BABY BEE

PARTY FLYERS & MORE

REMINISCENCES OF A UNIQUE ERA
IN BELGIAN NIGHTLIFE CULTURE

1993–2010

AfterClub

in loving memory of smos
(1967–2020)

FOREWORD	7
WE TALKED FOR HOURS	11
THEY WERE THERE	17
BLOKSKES & MORE	29
COMPILATIONS	29
FLYER ARCHIVE	33
1993 33	
1994 37	
1995 43	
1996 47	
1997 53	
1998 59	
1999 67	
2000 77	
2001 85	
2002 99	
2003 121	
2004 135	
2005 145	
2006 153	
2007 161	
2008 175	
2009 187	
DJ INDEX	195

FOREWORD

Sad news shook up our scene in April 2020: Smos had passed away. Aged 53, the Antwerp based DJ was a key figure of our Belgian nightlife scene. As yin to yang, Smos was connected to Baby Bee. The inseparable duo—who have been lovers as well—has rocked dance floors all over Belgium and abroad for 20 years of which 18 as resident DJs in Café d'Anvers and four in the Motion room in Fuse in Brussels. In July 1999 the influential UK's I-D Magazine awarded them DJ of the month and in 2001 they were entitled best Belgian DJs in the Ticket Nightlife awards. Having started their DJ career in the early nineties, their story is closely linked with the beginnings of Belgian DJ culture and the electronic music scene.

Although it feels much longer, I first met Baby Bee at Wally's Groove World in Antwerp about half a decade ago, can't recall the exact date. I have unfortunately never met Smos. As a house music fan and a DJ myself it feels like he has always been there though, as a televiewer acquainted with their favorite soap actors. Larger than life. By the end of the nineties, Smos and Baby Bee represented an alluring part of the world to me, slowly but surely revealing. As a young clubber trying to understand the culture they stood for, their name was oftentimes mentioned on the flyers, free magazines or posters I collected. I wanted to be alike, spend my life around the same records, with likeminded people, in venues with names that sounded important.

In April 2021 I requested an interview with Baby Bee. In the context of the content platform *Our Scene* that I had set up for Brussels' yearly Listen Festival, I wanted to share Smos and Baby Bee's story with the world, one year after the sudden death of Smos. Leaving behind many traces but not such a great deal in the digital spheres of the internet—a circumstance for many that have made their career in the years prior to the internet revolution—the time seemed right to reconstruct their legacy and share it with both a new audience and the older generations who witnessed the career of DJs Smos and Baby Bee at first hand.

Baby Bee agreed to the interview and we met in her apartment at Sint-Jacobsmarkt in Antwerp, at the time still the same as where she moved in with Smos in the early nineties. She spent almost three decades of her life in this flat, the longest anyone ever lived in the building famous for its legendary history. Bought by the owners of USA Import in 1979, José Pascual and Frie Verhelst, whose record shop had first opened in 1973 just a stone's throw away but with a growing business needed a bigger space, the flat on the second floor was rented out to befriended customers who were oftentimes also DJs or had other close involvements. As a matter of fact, Baby Bee lived in the flat until October 2022, when she was requested to move out due to an imminent sale of the building. For her, moving house and simultaneously working on this book project was an emotional trip down memory lane, as you will surely understand while browsing through this book.

So I found myself seated on a sofa in Baby Bee's apartment and we talked. We talked for hours. And although our relationship at the time of the first interview was only just starting to deepen, Baby Bee gave me her all. She laughed and cried, she told heart-warming stories and revealed difficult moments, she showed vulnerability and pride. Not much later, the result of our conversation was published on the website of Listen Festival. A version recently re-edited by Baby Bee and myself is also presented in this book.

By the end of our conversation, Baby Bee showed me 15 folders. Each had a time period written on a little name tag. In them she had collected every single artwork, flyer or poster of every party, event, club or festival Smos and Baby Bee ever performed as DJs. I was astonished. As a nightlife researcher and digger I have seen a few archives and collections already, but such a wealth of information so well preserved over the years is rather unique. As you will notice in the stories of people close to Smos and Baby Bee collected in this book, I'm not the only one who has been pleased with the pragmatic and organizational talents of Baby Bee.

After the first publication of the interview and the positive feedback it had triggered, I proposed the idea of a book to Baby Bee. Pushing forward the legacy of Smos and Baby Bee was important, I argued.

> 'The world deserves your story printed on paper and you do as well.'

Baby Bee needed a moment to contemplate. As you might know already or you'll learn from those quoted in this book, she has never enjoyed too much spotlight. I continued my oration.

> 'You have been a DJ duo prominently rocking our scene since its dawn, shortly after the infamous second summer of love in the UK during the late 1980s and the rising of a new youth culture, a pivotal point in music history when under the spell of XTC a large audience started to become enthralled by the exciting new style of music coming from American cities such as Detroit and Chicago. You and Smos were a DJ duo, a constellation well known in our contemporary club scene but at the time truly rare. You were a female acting in a mostly male world. You were DJing all over the country and through your genuine approach and straight forward mentality bringing together scenes from Brussels, Ghent, Antwerp or Wallonia. Your visual archive generates an important cache of a culture that during those two decades has been going through ups and downs, but is still very much alive and kicking to this very day. And finally, let's make a book to remember Smos, who is missed by many and remains in our hearts forever. So, what do you say?'

She said yes.

Here we are.

Today I can honestly say that I have met Smos, somehow, somewhere, through all the stories that were shared by all these people that call him a great friend. I'm very proud to present to you this book, offering a unique insight into the world of Smos and Baby Bee and the roots of our Belgian electronic music scene.

Although Smos and Baby also frequently played in clubs and at parties abroad, we have focused only on Belgian artwork for this publication. And for those who know, Smos and Baby have had some alter egos that were used on a fair few occasions. We furthermore decided not to use their real names in this book, since they both want to be remembered as Smos and Baby Bee.

> Thank you for the music, S&BB!

Koen Galle—Founder of AfterClub
April, 2023

WE TALKED FOR HOURS

KG *I would like to start at the very beginning. How did you meet Smos?*

BB It was 1990, I was in my twenties and I met Smos at Cafee Zodiac in Ghent, a bar in De Heilige Geeststraat where I often hung out. I have so many fond memories of those days, Cafee Zodiac was the epicentre of a convivial community and we were all so drawn into music, practising DJ skills and playing long sets night after night. It's in Cafee Zodiac that the name Baby B was coined because I always opted for the B-sides of records in pursuit of my favourite bonus beats or dub mixes. Later I changed my name to Baby Bee to get rid of a German DJ who claimed to have invented the name. Smos has always been Smos, he never wanted anyone to know his real name. He was always *smos-ing* around, a Flemish slang expression modified from the word *morsen* that means *to spill*. He actually took his nickname Smos from his favourite snack, a layered sandwich that is *smossy* to eat as it's difficult to avoid dropping pieces and messing around.

KG *What was it like in the nineties? What was on your mind those days?*

BB In November 1989 the Berlin wall had fallen and it made a lasting impression all over the world. In springtime 1990 with a few friends I drove all the way to Berlin, we wanted to witness what was going on there. I still have a small piece of the wall, taken as a souvenir of that historical moment. The wall killed so many people, it was a symbol of suppression and division. When it fell, it opened not only German borders and united their country, it symbolically put an end to the oppressive eighties and marked the start of a new decade.

The nineties were about some kind of awakening, renaissance of the youth counterculture and euphoria, not only in a hedonistic manner. You could also see it in the way people were dressed in those days, a comfortable sporty style was widely being accepted. T-shirts with a yellow smiley—a symbol that perfectly expressed the new mood—and comfortable sport shoes were very trendy, well describing the liberating, bright vibe of the new decade. Something new was happening all over Europe, the second *summer of love* was entering the youth culture after about 30 years since it first appeared in the memorable sixties. Perhaps the intro to Primal Scream's legendary *Loaded* remixed by Andrew Weatherhall describes best the nineties vibe: '[...] *we wanna be free to do what we wanna do, we wanna get loaded and we wanna have a good time.*'

KG *Where did you find your first musical kicks?*

BB In the early nineties there were a lot of parties going on in and around Ghent, mostly small and privately organised at special venues. I was really impressed by the vibe and music. My father was a jazz collector and although I have listened to a wide variety of music genres in the eighties, Jazz has always had a special place in my heart. When house music started to thrive I mostly fell for its more soulful and warmer Balearic style. To find the records that I heard at parties demanded a great effort and dedication because the new style of music was available strictly in specialised record shops, it was far away from the mainstream. The sense of secrecy and the fact that it was very difficult to find records in that style gave it a special charm. That's when my vinyl addiction began.

Due to connections of my employer in those days I often had to travel for work to London and I quickly indulged in its vast record shops that were mainly located in Soho. Thanks to one of my London based colleagues I also got to know the underground party scene. The city's nightlife was flourishing and I was lucky to get a chance to party in the legendary Shoom and at the *Boy's Own* parties, to hear DJs Andrew Weatherall, Terry Farley, Pete Heller, Danny Rampling and Carl Cox, and to experience the unique atmosphere of those pioneering house party years across the channel. Mind you, to enter Shoom was about as difficult as to get into Berghain. What Sven Marquardt is to Berghain, Rampling's wife Jenni was to Shoom. She kept very strict control of the audience and many people in the long waiting line would be refused entry. It was a kind of privilege to be accepted to get in. The club was located in Southwark Street, it had a rather small capacity of about 300 people. Once you entered the club, the vibe was incredible.

During the nineties Smos and I would often make day trips to London, taking the first ferry boat connection from Ostend in the early morning and coming back late in the evening, loaded with kilos of precious exciting new records and empty pockets. In Belgium we regularly bought records in the Music Man shop in Ghent and, of course, in the USA Import shop in Antwerp.

KG *Do you remember your first DJ set?*

BB Definitely! Smos and I teamed up with Smos' best friend Dirk De Ruyck—who later started the famous *Eskimo* parties and the Eskimo Recordings label—for a gig in Pacific in Antwerp. Run by Philip De Liser, this was a concert hall and club where DJs and live acts such as Lee Scratch Perry, Wizards of Ooze, Souls Asylum and Moondog performed. We mainly played acid jazz on that night, it was our first DJ set ever for a bigger audience. While we were living in Ghent, we were regularly playing at Zodiak alongside good friends Mo & Benoelie, who later changed their name to The Glimmer Twins. In 1992 I found a job in Antwerp and we decided to move.

KG *How did you become residents at Café d'Anvers?*

BB Koenie and Steve Cop were the first DJ residents in Café d'Anvers who established the new music policy in the club. When they quit in 1993, we took over their place together with Steve's younger brother Kenneth Cop. First I was booked by Kenneth, who liked my deep and dubby house style, to play together with him on Sunday nights. When we were soon promoted to Saturdays, Smos joined us with his energetic style heavily influenced by disco and funk that became indispensable for Café d'Anvers. The three of us were a great match behind the DJ booth and until 1996 we shared decks on our memorable eight hours long Saturday night sessions. After Kenneth had left the club, me and Smos continued to perform our monthly all night Saturday sessions until 2010, when I decided to stop DJing. Smos stayed in Café d'Anvers almost until its closing, in 2017 he celebrated the 25th anniversary of his DJ residency in the club.

KG *Can you describe what the Belgian scene looked like in the nineties?*

BB Café D'Anvers in Antwerp was the Belgian temple of house music. La Rocca in nearby Lier was also beginning with a new music style policy, but their DJs played a more commercial style. In the late nineties Red & Blue, Fill Collins and Club Geluk were opened in Antwerp. We belonged to a house scene, parallel with ours were the techno and trance oriented scenes with clubs such as Extreme, Cherry Moon and Fuse.

Brussels was rather quiet in the early nineties. Mirano is a veteran club in the Brussels's nightlife scene, but only in the mid nineties they started to program house music. DJs at the famous gay party *La Demence*, that was held in the same building where Fuse was established in 1994, also accepted the new style in the early nineties. I remember a few wild parties that were held at special locations in the capital, especially the parties in the Vaudeville theatre in Galerie de la Reine were memorable. Pablo Disco Bar was a small bar in the centre of Brussels where you could hear good house music and Who's Who Land opened in 1998. In a former grain silo in Leuven the *Food* parties started in 1996, where the best deep house DJs from all over the world were gracing the decks. Besides the famous techno room, Fuse also opened the Motion house room on the first floor, where we were residents for about four years between 2000 and 2004. It was an honour and pleasure to play in Fuse, I have fond memories of those days. Reminiscing of our DJing at Rue Blaes reminds me of my dear friend DJ St-Dic, another resident of Fuse, who sadly passed away in December 2006.

The third point in the Belgian party triangle is Ghent. After the closing of the famous Boccaccio located in nearby Destelbergen in 1993, you could hear house music only in Cafee Zodiac. In the early nineties I remember that we were going to 55 in Kuurne near Kortrijk, a club that was run by Peter Decuypere, who later started Fuse. The closing party of 55 was a legendary night. The *Eskimo* parties were a breakthrough for the Ghent club scene, those were very well organised parties with large rooms where various styles of music were played. The parties were set in the former Eskimo underwear factory and the audience was incredible. We always played the closing hours in the house room for a few thousand enthusiastic party people, it was a memorable experience. The legendary *Eskimo* parties were later on continued with the *Bel Mondo* parties held in S.M.A.K. and in other special locations, followed by the opening of Culture Club and Make-Up.

KG *What was your magical formula as a DJ duo?*

BB Playing back-to-back surely needed some experience, it took a while before we learned how to master the skill. Our playing was not planned ahead but rather pure improvising, variety and surprises were always a special spice of our sets. Someone once told me that our magic was in the fact that I was playing for girls and Smos for boys, a guaranteed formula to get everyone on the dance floor. As a woman I certainly had a female touch and Smos was the masculine side, but the magic was in balancing and bridging our differences. While I've always preferred a deeper, jazzy, spaced out and dubby groove, Smos was into solid fat-bass funk and uplifting disco. The symbiosis of our styles somehow seemed to work very well.

We always had an agreement to each play a mini set of three records, which we called *blokskes*. These small blocks of about 10 to 15 minutes allowed us to keep the groove going in a smooth way. In a packed Café d'Anvers, in the main room of 10 Days Off, in the Motion room of Fuse, at the Eskimo parties, at the Rex club in Paris or anywhere else we played, it was quite a responsibility to keep the vibe alive and people dancing until the late hours. The most important role of a DJ is to make people feel good, the selection of records in a live DJ set is not about ego tripping, it's really important to communicate with the audience and follow their reaction. Dance music is all about mixing, creating a story with a selection of records, feeding the audience with energy for their moving bodies, but also their mind and soul. The record is on average played for about 3–4 minutes, it is very important to think ahead,

Smos and Baby Bee at the City Parade in Ghent in 2004. | © Benoit Meeus

Smos and Baby Bee at the City Parade in Ghent in 2004. | © Benoit Meeus

WE TALKED FOR HOURS

© Baby Bee

to plan your next move almost like playing chess. DJing with two has an advantage in this process. While Smos was playing I had more time to think about my choice for the next three records. Sometimes I felt like it was needed to inject more emotion or spacey tracks, other times I simply had to continue the energy flow. The choice of records is essential, but so is the technical skill, the way of bringing the tracks in. Give a few records to various DJs, they will all mix them in a different way, and that is the unique quality of DJing. Yes, it's literally all in the mix.

I remember how Smos on a couple of occasions took the needle from the playing turntable. All of a sudden there was no more sound. He was kind of paralysed and all eyes pointed on us. I shouted 'drop it!' and he would then literally do that, drop the needle on the spinning record. Imagine the energy going through the room when the crowd was faced with an unexpected silence, followed by a few quick pops of the needle while falling down, after which the groove would take off again in full swing.

We always spent at least a couple of hours preparing a selection of records for our set. None of our sets were ever fully preprogrammed, something that is becoming rather common in today's much bigger and more commercialised party scene. We thrived on spontaneity, interaction with the crowd and we were often dancing behind the booth. Playing an all night set in Café d'Anvers was especially by all means demanding. As a rule we would each take two big record boxes plus a bag with about 50 specials to avoid playing the same record twice during the night. Eight-hour sets enabled us to play different styles during the night: deeper in the beginning, full energy in the mid part and spacey after-hours style in the last part. The choice of the last record was a special moment. Like a signature, this was the DJ statement to round off the night, a track that stays in the clubber's memory after leaving the dancefloor. We both had a few records in our boxes especially reserved for the last tune.

KG *How did a week in the lives of Smos & Baby Bee look like in those roaring nineties?*

BB From the early nineties until 2010 we truly lived with, for and from music. Besides DJing we both worked in record stores. Smos was active at USA Import and I worked at Wally's Groove World, the latter opening in 1997 as a second-hand record shop in the basement of USA Import. When the apartment above the shop became vacant, we did not hesitate to move in. Even though it was in the same building where we both worked and therefore convenient, it wasn't always a matter of great comfort. The wooden floor didn't cancel any noise coming from the shop, but since we were both working there anyway it did not bother us that much. Unless we tried to catch some sleep on Saturday morning after a long night of playing.

During the weekend—sometimes starting on Thursday and going on until Monday morning— we were DJing and often coming home at dawn. On Sunday and Monday we were usually recovering from nightlife's side effects and having an easy day. If the weekend wasn't too busy, we often ended our Sundays with a recording session cooking up new mixes on cassettes. They were especially in the nineties highly in demand. We often took a dozen copies to parties where we were DJing and gave them away. Tapes were our promotional tool in the days before the internet. On Tuesdays Smos would start his working week in USA Import while I still had a free day. Thursdays and Fridays were record shopping days, when fresh vinyl supply arrived in the shops. On Friday afternoons all shops were full of DJs and record collectors who were hungry for the new releases. We were lucky to have the first choice thanks to Smos's job. Working in the record shop was crucial to success as a DJ in those days. There was a limited number of copies ordered, so you had to be lucky to get something you liked as there was a kind of hierarchy. DJs who had a residency or played a lot had a privilege above other DJs.

When we had a residency in the Motion room in Fuse, I was often going to visit the Doctor Vinyl shop in Brussels for another pile of new records and precious white label promos given to me by Geert Sermon, the shop's owner.

KG *Did you and Smos share records? What were the dynamics between the two of you, how do you remember him?*

BB I remember him as a truly good-hearted person, we spent many happy years together. He was an energy ball, a *jolly joker* type that could sometimes turn into a *Tasmanian Devil* cartoon character. Until about 2011 there was a total trust in our relationship, from then on we were unfortunately falling apart and we broke up in 2013. Although our general backgrounds and tastes in music were rather different, we gladly learned from each other and enriched each other's knowledge. Yes, there was always his and my stuff, but we often shared what we played. Only occasionally we bought the same record twice, mainly as a safety spare copy.

KG *Can you describe the importance of vinyl records in those days?*

BB DJing was quite a challenging job that demanded investing a lot of time in shopping and searching for records. The nightlife's tempo and carrying heavy boxes full of records was for sure not an easy part, I know a few DJ friends who have serious injuries on their backs. In this pre-internet, pre-digital era you were simply obliged to buy plenty of records to be able to play a good set. White label promos were especially precious because they guaranteed the exclusivity in playing a top track before anyone else could get it. Someone invented the term vinyl mafia for DJs who were covering record labels with stickers or deleting info on promos to prevent other DJs getting to know them. Honestly speaking we were all doing it, finding a good record was the result of hard work and endlessly digging in specialised record shops. For a very long time in my life everything was measured by the basic price of a record. For example, if I wanted to buy a new pair of shoes, I compared the price with the number of records I could buy for the same amount.

KG *You own a RODEC, a legendary Belgian brand of DJ mixers known for their superior sound quality, durability and ease of use. Was this the quintessential Smos and Baby Bee mixer?*

BB In February 1994 we hosted a night at Chic at Ketelvest in Ghent. At the time we were plotting to move to London, where I had lived before and still had a lot of friends. Counting the proceedings of the party, we became unsure of our plan though. London was an expensive city and the event hadn't turned as profitable as we hoped it would. So in the end we decided to stay in Belgium and use the money to buy decent audio equipment. We went to Arton in Antwerp, a now defunct shop at Sint-Katelijnevest, in those days a very important place for DJ culture. The RODEC mixer would never leave our house again and is very much part of our identity.

KG *Was it hard to get around as a female DJ in a world dominated by males?*

BB Not really, it didn't stop or restrict me from doing what I wanted to do. In Belgian shops everyone knew us, but in some record shops abroad the owners and assistants were the macho type and would not easily accept a female customer. When they would realise that I knew quite something about music, they would soften their arrogant attitude. I can especially remember this happening in San Francisco in 2000. Record shopping in Berlin has always been a wonderful experience, and I can say the same about Rotterdam, London and Cologne, where we often travelled for record shopping.

In the nineties there were only 3 professional female DJs in Belgium to my knowledge: Trish, D'Stephanie and me. It was quite demanding on a physical level to live the nightlife, carry heavy boxes and frequently visit various record shops to get new records. It needed financial sacrifice to buy records and essential DJ equipment, Since most of the DJs were male, young women didn't have many role models to look up to. Happily this is changing now with many strong female DJs taking a position at the top.

KG *How do you perceive the changes the DJ scene has gone through during your long career spanning both the nineties and the two thousands?*

BB In hindsight the nineties were defined by the fact that we didn't have the internet or mobile phones, computers were still in development, music was produced analog, there was no digital files overload nor easy online shopping. It was a real endeavour to get the records you wanted and we spent so much time physically visiting shops. About three quarters of our income went to record stores. Magazines such as the UK's Jockey Slut, DJ Magazine and Mixmag or Belgian Out Soon and Plastics were a really important source for information about the new releases and what was happening in the scene.

By the end of the nineties the entry of the euro currency led to the start of a new era, boosting the scene by easy travelling thanks to open European borders. Suddenly it was much easier to play abroad and getting paid in a foreign currency wasn't a hassle anymore. You could really feel things were taken to a more professional level in those days. The feeling of freedom we felt just after the introduction of the euro was comparable to what happened after the fall of the Berlin wall. Apple's iMac and the rise of the internet and social networking like Myspace also allowed our DJ scene to grow. We were finally able to make a bit more money and organise things on a bigger scale.

By the end of the nineties it had taken us a lot of effort to find a bookkeeper who was able to help us officially declare our income as professional DJs, since a DJ performance was not yet registered as a profession. After 2000 things in Belgium started to slowly but surely change and with it also the scale of events. Another evolution in the same period was the start of booking agencies. The first booking agency where we were accepted was set up by the Food party management. They promoted Belgian DJs such as Koenie, Geoffroy and Raoul from Food, St. Dic, Pierre, Trish and Deg from Fuse and Morpheus, D'Stephanie and Smos and me.

Sadly in 2001 the terror attacks on the Twin Towers in New York happened, bringing another burden to our lives. All of the sudden the whole world got scared and everyone was a suspect and the US ignited the *war on terror*. It didn't change the sense of how we partied, but it did change how we travelled. Some customs officers gave you the hardest time checking all your stuff at the airport.

KG *You concluded your DJ career in 2010 while Smos continued to DJ for another nine years. What made you decide to put an end to it?*

BB I've put a lot of effort into my almost 20-years-long DJ career with Smos, but I've never stopped having other interests. Before I got into DJing I had graduated at university and got my master's degree, but in the mid nineties I gave up my work to fully focus on our DJ career. Near the end of 2000 I started to feel the burden of nightlife, the spark of excitement was somehow fading away and I felt like trying something else and pursuing other goals. Besides the physical difficulties related to the nightlife job, I did not like the upscaling and expansion of our scene. More and more people were investing in it for profit, more is more became the rule. The rise of many big parties and festivals was often focused not on quality, but quantity. We frequently had technical issues that would make it difficult to comfortably work and enjoy it. After many such frustrating occasions I decided to leave the DJ scene. Last time I played in Café d'Anvers was at the New Year's party in 2010. It was an emotional moment, but I've never regretted stopping my career because I was determined to do something else in my life. After my DJ period I studied photography and graphic design that helped me to find work in that direction.

KG *How do you look back at the end of your partnership with Smos?*

BB Our break-up as a couple was not easy because our lives were entangled on so many levels in the period of two decades of our DJ career. Just after the separation there was a crisis in our relationship, but soon we again became good friends. The fatal year 2020 was very difficult in many ways, his sudden death deeply affected me. Strange as it is, Smos passed away on the day of my birthday. The two of us were for a very long time closely connected, we've known each other for 30 years. The mysterious strings of life kept us together until the end of his life. I will always dearly remember him.

© Baby Bee

THEY WERE THERE

JAMILA DE BACKER

Smos and I go way back. We met more than 30 years ago in Ghent and even lived together for a while. We often hung out at Zodiac, a small bar and club where a bunch of like minded people and DJs spent many days and nights together. We were young and wild. I studied photography at the Royal Academy of Fine Arts, he was into disco and seventies music; we all had something going on.

Later we both moved to Antwerp. Those were the nineties, I worked at Café d'Anvers, he was the DJ and he often came to say hello or keep company. Smos knew what my most favorite tunes were and that once they hit the speakers, I would come running to him. His music and the way he danced, had a way of touching my soul. Our group of friends was very close.

What made our friendship so special was the highest level of trust between us. We could be completely ourselves in each other's company without feeling like having to live up to something or pretending to be better. He was one of the nicest friends I've ever had, the sort of person who always made me happy just because I was thinking about him. If I looked at my phone and saw that I had a text from him, I would immediately smile. I picture his face in my head and smile just thinking of his smile.

I truly miss him. His passing makes me feel vulnerable. Our friendship was something special and lasted even after I left nightlife and Antwerp and found a day-time job. After all these years, we still felt the urge to spend time together. I still do feel that now.

Smos in the early nineties. | © Jamila De Backer

PIERRE NOISIEZ

Smos and I first connected in the very beginning of the nineties, when I was 18 or 19 years old. We were both making our first steps as a DJ and were also often going out together, usually ending up at his apartment close to Dampoort in Ghent to play records and chat until the morning sun. Although in the later stages of our lives we were never able to spend as much time together as we did in those years, this was the start of a great friendship. A bit later Baby Bee appeared in Smos's and our lives.

We all shared the same taste for deep and American house music, released on labels such as Nervous or Nu Groove. Or the Dutch stuff, disco music or Detroit techno. I was the first to start playing at Café d'Anvers, where I was invited in 1992 or 1993 by Koenie to become a resident DJ alongside Charles Schilling, Steve Cop and Koenie himself. We played on Sunday nights, which soon became a special and legendary night. Not much later Smos and Baby Bee also started playing in Café d'Anvers.

In 1994 Fuse in Brussels opened and I started playing there as a resident DJ. In Fuse I turned more towards techno music, while they remained on their house trip. We still crossed paths quite often but we were all occupied and had less free time to spend together. I remember seeing Baby Bee mostly at Wally's Groove World when I went digging for records.

DIRK DERUYCK

Smos, Tom Derie and I were a triumvirate living in Ghent around the end of the eighties and early nineties. We shared a passion for the same type of music and its coinciding subcultures and movements. We were strongly inspired by what happened across the channel, where indie, acid jazz, dance, ... was all part of a vibrant scene while we at the time started to discard the overly exploited New Beat records. We all bought an insane amount of vinyl records.

In Ghent our nightlife was centered around Zodiac, a local bar that on weekends was transformed into a cozy club for about 150 people. The venue soon gained national attention with people coming from everywhere. These were truly formative years for a scene that was still tiny at the time. Looking back at Zodiac now, I believe the club was a true pioneer for being a safe place for the LGBTQ+ community and an example of what nightlife would later become in our city cultures.

Smos was the most avid DJ among us, completely obsessed with DJing and collecting records. We spent a lot of time with DJ Pierre or Charles Chillings and went to Café d'Anvers every Sunday evening to hear DJ Koenie play.

We met Baby Bee in Zodiac and all became friends. A few weeks later Baby Bee and Smos fell in love and would later move to Antwerp, while I started working for *La Demence* in Brussels for a few years. After a short break from nightlife and a job in the music industry, I co-founded the *Eskimo* parties in 1997. These were a huge success and led to the creation of the *Bel Mondo* parties in SMAK, Club 69 and Culture Club among others, all now part of nightlife history in Ghent. Smos and Baby Bee were part of all these right from the start.

A PLAYLIST FROM THOSE
DAYS IN GHENT:

David Byrne & Brian Eno—*The Carrier*
A Man Called Adam—*Techno Powers*
Fingers Inc.—*Music Takes Me Up*
Mission Control—*Outta Limits* (Shelter Mix)
Bobby Konders—*Massai Woman*
Primal Scream—*Don't Fight It, Feel It*
KC Flight—*Planet E* (Acid Drop Mix)
DV8—*Freedom* (In Deep Mix)
QX1—*I Won't Hurt You (I Swear)*
Basil Hardhaus—*Make Me Dance (Hard for the DJ)*

STEVE COP

I started to get to know them better when they moved in the flat above USA Import, the now closed record shop in Antwerp, where Smos also worked as a store clerk. Our paths had already crossed several times at parties or through friends in common, but from that point on we became good friends. Both Smos and Baby Bee were extremely passionate and intensely involved in their jobs as DJs and music selectors. They belong, just as a few other DJs from that generation, to the true pioneers of nightlife in Belgium. I'm delighted to call them friends.

DAVE BRODY

We were a lot together at Café d'Anvers, since I was the light jockey there for 18 years. I met Smos & Baby Bee before I started to work at Café d'Anvers and saw them both regularly in the nightlife. Years later when I was working at the USA Records studio we became closer, again through music. One day Smos asked me if I would like to do lights at Café d'Anvers. The weekend after, with zero experience, I started there and we became colleagues to burn the dance floor.

In those years Smos had more than a few incidents, losing his jacket, shoes and more, forgetting his record bag and headphones... Close encounters with people, the dreadful doormen... We partied hard, had big fun, some incidents which most of the time led to big laughs afterwards.

You see, Smos always saw a way to get spirits up and the way he played was unique, entertaining and funky as can be, I can't emphasize enough on that. How he brought his set, pushing energy or keeping it back when needed, adding fades and soaring the mix, Smos added his soul and musical knowledge and played in his own way. That vibe reflected on the dance floor and I saw people going 100% in or even going mad, turning people into animals as they said in Café. Personally he made me a better person and light jockey. I like to remember him this way, musically trying to push the envelope and good laughs to accompany with.

RAOUL BELMANS

I first met Smos and Baby Bee at Café d'Anvers in 1993. Attracted by the new and exciting sounds played in the nightclub, my first visits at the age of 19 were a genuine revelation. Although at first I didn't really know who was playing these amazing records, DJs weren't put on a pedestal as they are now, I soon realized Smos and Baby Bee were among the DJs often at work there.

On my quest for American house records, I also set foot at USA Import, the record store where Smos was working and where he and Baby Bee lived on the second floor. Smos really was an excellent store clerk, the best at selling records. 'I've got something great here for you', he used to say enthusiastically while doing a little dance to prove his point. Their apartment always had open doors, I remember spending plenty of hours there just chatting or listening to more records. It was cozy and very well decorated, in a seventies vibe. At that time I started to get to know Baby Bee much better. She was more timid and organized, while Smos was always playing around and very extraverted.

By around 1996 I became a resident DJ at Food in Leuven, where we often shared the decks. We also regularly traveled abroad for gigs, always resulting in fun trips low on sleep but high on energy. You could count the house DJs in Belgium on two hands at the time, so we shared many line-ups during those years. Other colleagues were Koenie, Geoffroy, St. Dic, Frederik, Bart, Mo & Benoelie and Bernard Dobbeleer.

When Koenie started his record shop Wally's Groove World, I often joined him on digging trips. His strategy was as simple as it was effective: he invited a bunch of DJs with him on the trip and paid for our hotel and food. We rented a van and drove around Europe. As a result I ended up in Hamburg, London or Milan spending days in warehouses stacked with records. Smos and Baby Bee were also regulars on those trips.

Reminiscing about my time with Smos, I remember him as one of the most positive minded human beings I have ever met. Even when beset by troubles, he would show a happy face. His presence was infectious, just as his DJ sets were. Seeing Smos and Baby Bee deejay together was very inspiring, a DJ duo wasn't very common back then. They were true DJs, pur sang, for the love of the music and among the colleagues that truly inspired me.

Baby Bee definitely also pioneered as a female DJ in a male world. Calling her the mother of Belgian house is maybe a bit too far-fetched, but she always had some kind words or good advice in store for me. She was a silent yet essential force, both in duo with Smos as in our national house scene.

PHILIP DE LISER

I mainly knew Smos & Baby Bee as employees of USA Import where I spent ridiculous amounts of time (and money). What mainly characterized them both was their positive attitude and a certain 'joie de vivre'. Smos was always the playful bird and Baby Bee the more serious and dutiful.

That was also noticeable during their DJ sets: Baby Bee meticulously put together her sets time after time while Smos was more likely to *go with the flow*. That combo seemed to work.

I have booked them various times for 10 Days Off, where they fitted well as they were true banging house DJs. It must be mentioned that Baby Bee was probably one of the first female Belgian DJs. I believe she started around the same time as DJ Stephanie?

A few days before Smos' passing, in the middle of the corona lockdown, I ran into Smos. It was a very nice, relaxed conversation. He was still overflowing with enthusiasm and zest for life. Dear and kind-hearted people, forever Smos & Baby Bee!

GEOFFROY DEWANDELER

My first encounter with DJs Smos & Baby Bee was around the early nineties, when Pia from the Closing Date shop and Sebastiano hosted parties in Antwerp. Those parties had a secretive and exclusive kinda vibe, held in small underground venues for a very nicely dressed up crowd and strictly centered around vocal American house and garage music. Smos & Baby Bee were really into that vibe and played those sorts of parties. That scene was small and everybody knew each other. A lot of friends of mine in Brussels went to these events and raved about their DJ skills. We eventually met later but this was before they started playing in Café d'Anvers. My old friend Fifi started to book them at his parties in the Vaudeville in Brussels where I also played and he then also ran nights in Café d'Anvers with Detroit DJs and Belgian guests like us. Later I often played in Flanders, so over the years we shared many line-ups and nightly experiences, including through my enduring DJ residency with Raoul at *Food* in Silo in Leuven and later in Brussels.

In the early nineties, after having worked at the store of USA Import in Brussels with Poltergeist, the first deep house DJ in Belgium who was also known from legendary parties in Brussels with New York legend Mark Kamins, Italian legend Ricci Montanari or the young Sven Väth, I kinda graduated and started working at Wally's Groove World in Antwerp for Koenie who was one the original Café d'Anvers residents. His shop was at the time located in the basement of USA Import in Antwerp. Smos and Baby Bee lived in the flat above the store and also worked in both record stores. I spent a lot of time with them. We had access to many imports and new titles that were hard to find. Holding such a position was really important in the pre-internet age. Most of the key DJs at the time were working in record shops, for distributors or labels.

Smos was a really good DJ, very open minded and enthusiastic. He was a really good record seller too. He was always very caring, a party guy but not too much. Baby Bee wanted to have things tidy and steady and was always looking for the perfect beat. They both were obsessed with the records and extremely serious about the craft, the job and the ethos of creative DJing. They matched together very well.

Vaudeville, April 1993.

BRANDY VOLANT

I first invited Smos & Baby Bee to play at club Rêve d'Ô in Tournai around 1995. During the following two years they were regular guests at my residency in Catacombes in Roeselare. Between 1998 and 2004 they headlined more at Rêve d'Ô, when the club relocated to Barry. In this part of Belgium mostly known for its Trance and Progressive house music, we were the first club to only have house music on the bill.

They represented house music in an eclectic, joyful and overall quality spirit. Together with Stefaan Vandenberghe aka T-Quest, they were my main source of inspiration. They teached me to play records out of the ordinary and as a result strongly influenced my style as a DJ. Every Thursday my friend Kalky and I drove all the way to Antwerp to listen to the new records at USA Import and Wally's Groove World, where we often hung out with them.

I was honored to put out two EPs on Wally's Groove World's label in 1998 and 1999; my relationship with Smos & Baby Bee surely has played a role here. Later, Smos mentioned *Walk On The 5th Avenue* as one of his three favorite house music tracks in an interview alongside music by Telex and Spirit Catcher. It's the best compliment someone has ever given to me.

JANE HAESEN
Lady Jane

As a young DJ and student living in Antwerp, I visited USA Import and Wally's Groove World often. To be able to get a hold of the good records, you had to get along well with the store clerk, for them to keep copies of the good stuff aside. Smos and I became good friends.

I remember visiting the ground floor apartment he lived in with Baby Bee, close to the Meir. Entering their place was like entering another universe, decorated with bright colors, vintage orange plastic design objects, soft carpets, beautiful furniture, … all inspired by flower power and the seventies. I immediately felt at home.

As an adolescent I was rather shy and insecure. But their kindness made me overcome these insecurities. The same goes for all these nights in Café d'Anvers and the community in the club at the time. We all enjoyed this exciting new music together, it was very liberating.

Smos and Baby Bee were a fitting DJ duo. Their styles were slightly different, but came together in a unique blend. Smos was always smiling and had a very energetic style of DJing, his music selection was often infused by a disco groove. *Double Dutch Bus* by Frankie Smith, a record from 1981, is a track that I will always connect to Smos. I owned a house remix, he taught me the original version. Baby Bee's selection was a tiny bit darker, she was more influenced by techno music I guess.

WARD VAN DEN BOGERD
Veebo

When I first moved to Antwerp, I lived just a stone's throw away from Smos. We often hung out, went skating or threw the frisbee. Or we spent time together in the music studio at USA Import, where Smos also lived in the apartment on the second floor. So it happened that somewhere around the year 2010, we were spontaneously recording an analog driven moody house jam. I recall Smos was in control of a SH101 and a Juno 60 that night and with flair and enthusiasm he tweaked the filter cutoff throughout the track. We never really did something with the resulting track, besides playing it out loud a few times. I remember walking into the Avenue Sneaker Shop where Smos worked a few months later when he told me: 'Ward, we need to call this track *The Whistler* as I'm always whistling along'.

I'm thankful to Smos for all the frisbees, chill sessions, spontaneous party nights, race bikes, introducing me to the music of Jovonn, sharing the decks and so much more.

GEERT SERMON
Doctor Vinyl Brussels

I have always been proud that Smos & Baby Bee came to visit Doctor Vinyl on a regular basis, while they worked and lived in and above a record shop in Antwerp. Their dedication to finding the best new music for their DJ sets was far beyond the tour of duty. Baby Bee was really a regular, she was part of the Doctor Vinyl family. She bought most of her off kilter stuff at ours, records that weren't available in Antwerp and we were able to offer her. She treated records almost as a librarian, with great care and precision. Doctor Vinyl has always been a bit wild and messy, but Baby Bee applied some kind of chirurgical approach to this, always finding exactly those records she needed.

Baby Bee always used to visit us on Friday at noon, if it wasn't weekly at least biweekly. Smos also frequented the shop, but much less. When he traveled to Brussels for record shopping, he mostly visited Urban Grooves. Sometimes they called asking us to keep a record aside. Not for themselves, but for a befriended foreign DJ such as Frenchman D'Julz who was in town and was desperate to also get a copy of the record.

What united all of us in my tiny shop in the center of Brussels, was the Motion Room at Fuse. This upstairs and cozy second area of the club was where the records we listened to during the week were being played for crowds on Friday and Saturday nights. These years, when DJs St. Dic and Frederik were residents alongside Smos and Baby Bee, are now often referenced as the golden years of the Motion Room.

COLIN MCBREAN
Mr. G

I was invited to play at Café d'Anvers somewhere in the nineties, when I met Smos and Baby Bee. It was the start of a different chapter. We really got along together with our shared deep love for music. Whether we were playing, chatting or digging, we all were exchanging and learning from each other. To be fair they were both great DJs and like all in life we had our ups and downs.

This was the middle of the nineties and I was making music and they also chose to make music with my help and ears whenever they needed me. It was crazy really if you look back at it now, as they were so ahead of the game with the art side Baby Bee had. Life was fun back then.

I have so many souvenirs here at home, stuff they sent me that still pops up now and then and reminds me of a great point in life.

As we all grew up I still kept in contact with Smos sadly I didn't know he had passed as my messages stopped in April 2020. Steve Cop told me when I came to play my first gig after the covid pandemic in Brussels, heartbreaking news. I miss them both to be fair.

JAN VAN BIESEN

We were often lined up at parties in a consecutive order. Taking over from them or leaving the DJ booth to them, our encounters were always very warm-hearted. I remember them as a beautiful couple, always smiling and adding a great share of energy into any party, even to the point that I was a bit starstruck when we first met. They both had a natural flair and some kind of mundane attitude, not at all snobby but simply honest and affectionate.

They didn't bullshit around, but were straight forward DJs with a positive attitude and an open mindedness unique in the scene. Baby Bee was extremely focused as a DJ, you could see she knew exactly what she was doing and was always in full control. Smos was a real natural, a funkateer, who could surprise you at any given moment with great panache. Their record crates had this mystical aura. Much more than my own, theirs were truly a holy grail, a bag full of gold.

I often invited them in my radio shows at Studio Brussel, especially in Switch, a show that helped emancipate underground electronic music on national radio. We broadcasted every Friday and Saturday for seven hours and Smos and Baby Bee performed multiple guest mixes.

Shit Goddamn, a track they did under their Raw alter ego for Eighttrack Recordings, had a fixed position in my DJ bag for quite a while. It was a great set opener and often made it into my radio playlists. I also included it in the tracklist of *Full Bass 3 – Future House Grooves From Belgium*, a compilation I made in 1999.

The last time I met Smos was at Café Capital in Antwerp, where we shared a line-up in September 2019. We had met a few days before the party to talk with a journalist from Het Laatste Nieuws, reminiscing about our shared past. It was a great night and he still truly excelled in DJing, but afterwards firmly told me was going to quit nightlife. Serenely he admitted he had lost touch, I found it hard to believe. Unfortunately he passed away not much after.

Raw, *Shit Goddamn*;
Eighttrack Recordings, Antwerp, 1999.

FILIP VAN MOERKERCKE
Filliz

Our roads clustered on many occasions. I first connected with them when I was shopping for records at USA Import or Wally's Groove World. In the early two thousands I started working for the latter, when the record store's sublabel Wha? Roots Recordings was about to release its first full album by the band Arsenal and Koenie needed help promoting it. I spent many hours close to the Sint-Jacobsmarkt and got to know them very well.

I was attracted by Baby Bee's cosmopolitan style. With her I discussed architecture, art, fashion, photography and music. She more or less took care of me as a sister figure, reprimanding me when I did something silly. Being a rather sloppy person I often mistreated my records, wrote on them, lost sleeves, … to the great despair of Baby Bee. She literally wanted to tidy up my record bag while I was mixing in the club. We had a lot of fun together.

In 2001 I started deejaying in Café d'Anvers as Filliz. We shared many line-ups over the years, I often witnessed them playing peak time. Smos was definitely the libertine among them while Branca was more serious. The resulting tension was what made them so good as a DJ duo. Baby Bee treated records the way an architect would, subtly and with great care and some sort of melancholy. Her skills and technique were flabbergasting. For instance, she started a record in the middle to emphasize a certain part of a track or she played a surprising B-side. To this, Smos would add his pure and raw energy, generating many out of the blue highlights. Their magic happened somewhere in the middle.

In 2002 I founded Café Capital together with two associates. I wanted to have Smos and Baby Bee on board as well, but in order not to offend Café d'Anvers where we had our residencies, they were programmed as DJs Elastix in Café Capital. Antwerp was big enough for two Café's and at Capital they could unleash their more eclectic music taste.

JULIEN VENIEL
D'Julz

Bass Culture at Rex Club, Paris, Saturday 12. 09. 1998.

A record offered by Baby Bee to D'Julz.

My first encounter with Smos & Baby Bee was on Tuesday December 24th 1996. The reason I remember the date is because of the party flyer Baby Bee kept in her archives and that is shown in this book, stunningly designed by the great illustrator Dadara, also known for the iconic artwork for Dutch house labels Spiritual and Outland Records. It was the first of many nights we shared the line-up, a *Paradise* party hosted by Patrick Soks in Café d'Anvers. Patrick had heard me play in Paris when we met through our friend in common Charles Schilling.

In 1997 I began hosting my own nights called *Bass Culture* in the Parisian Rex Club. The scene in France at the time was quite separated: you had those who played techno, those who played French touch, those who played American house, and so on. When I started playing, I wanted to mix all: UK Breakbeat with Italian house, Detroit techno or Chicago house. I quickly found my peers in Belgium and The Netherlands: DJs such as Koenie, Dimitri from Roxy or Frederik did the same. Really connecting well with the energy and diversity of their funky sets, from the start of *Bass Culture* Smos and Baby Bee also became regular guests.

The other way around, they kept on inviting me to Café d'Anvers or Fuse as well. We shared many line-ups and they also often invited me to reside in their flat in Antwerp, even when I was playing at parties that weren't theirs. I have fond memories of these weekends, when they prepared food for me and installed the bed in the music room surrounded by a wall of records. Since Smos worked at USA Import, I also touched upon the best records they had in store. They treated me so well, they are among the most wonderful people I have ever met in my entire life. I still regularly find records in my collection that they offered me. They had the habit of writing stuff on the sleeves and Baby Bee would often put little stickers on them.

FRIE VERHELST

Smos was one of our store clerks and an essential element in the success of USA Import in the second part of the nineties. He was officially hired on December 1st 1994 and worked for us until December 31st 2002. We already knew him as a customer, he was a welcome guest with whom I instantly connected well. When a position opened up behind the counter, he jumped on it. We didn't hesitate.

THEY WERE THERE

Smos was always in a jovial mood at work. He had a perfect work ethic and was always available to help customers in the best possible way. He was obsessed with records and music meant the world to him. His knowledge was impressive and his advice for ordering from the distributors helped us tremendously.

When the apartment on the second floor of the shop became available, Smos and Baby Bee started to rent it from us. This must have been in 1995 or 1996. Smos lived there until they broke up, Baby Bee stayed until 2022. They really made the place their own, a few people have occupied the space but they definitely left behind the most memories.

Even after his time as our employee or tenant, he kept on visiting the Sint-Jacobsmarkt. He sometimes used the music studio, or he set up a bike repair atelier in the basement for quite a while. Our daughter Daphne's bike was made by Smos and is truly indispensable to her. Our grandson Lucian's first cross bike was also manufactured by Smos. And my husband José is also a huge cycling fan and often spent hours with Smos working on custom-made bikes.

STÉPHANIE D'OLIESLAGER For years I played on Friday nights at Café d'Anvers as a resident DJ, while Smos & Baby Bee played on Saturdays and Sundays. I was off on Sundays, so me and a bunch of friends often went to the club to hear them play. We also spent a lot of time at their apartment—which I remember as a museum full of curiosities—listening to records or having long conversations. Music was our common denominator. Me and Baby Bee went along very well. She often cooked excellent food for me.

I'll never forget how musically well trained Baby Bee was. Smos and I were a bit more on the nonchalant side, while she could easily hear when we mixed for instance two tracks in different keys that for her didn't fit well. This could lead to hilarious situations between the three of us.

Their choice of house music was quite unique, a bit naive, very New York and Chicago, a tad dry but quite funky and always with an other-wordly twist. I was listening to a DJ mix by the contemporary New York based duo The Carry Nation, who reminded me of what Smos & Baby Bee used to do. I still love it.

PATRICK SOKS The first Paradise party I ever organized at Café d'Anvers was on the last day of October in 1991. The idea had grown on me during holidays in Ibiza, with my friend Peter Decuypere who at the time ran his club Fifty Five in Kuurne where I already hosted parties. The people behind Café d'Anvers invited me to host a night at their venue, hoping to attract new crowds and energy. 2000 people showed up and Paradise was born.

I hosted countless nights in Café d'Anvers in the nineties and usually on the first Sunday of the month: Paradise, Natural Elements or Soks Parties. And it didn't take long for Smos and Baby Bee to appear on my line-ups, alongside DJs such as Koenie, Kenneth and Steve Cop. They were among those DJs that understood the new music that was arriving at the time, coming from Ibiza, Detroit and Chicago. I even had dancers coming over from the famous Pacha club in Ibiza for my nights.

Smos and Baby Bee were unique in many ways. As a beautiful couple, since you didn't have DJ duos at the time. And they simply rocked the boat every time they played. Their choice of music was sublime, this was where we fully connected. We're talking about the actual beginning of the house scene, music that in the early nineties wasn't as known as it is today. Our scene was really underground back then. Not everyone was convinced of what we did, but we pushed through and we thoroughly enjoyed ourselves.

Those years were truly pivotal for a few reasons. There was this new music, but there was also the melting pot of creative souls coming from many directions. I specifically wanted to connect art and nightlife. For instance, I had some of my artwork made by the Dutch designer Dadara who I had discovered in Holland for his beautiful designs for

Paradise party token.

Outland and Spiritual Records. Or I hosted nights for fashion designers, for Dutch label Natural Elements or for Penthouse magazine. Everyone mixed and mingled.

In 2016, some years after Smos and Baby Bee had parted ways, they were so kind to collaborate one more time to co-create the DJ mix for the compilation album I released celebrating 25 years of Paradise. Rest assured, they didn't lose their skills.

FLORIS MACHIELS
Hill Men

I am much younger and haven't experienced the heydays of Smos and Baby Bee. But I did get to know Baby Bee very well over the past few years. *Tante B*—as I like to call her—always has so many great stories to share about her DJ adventures all over the world. Every time we meet—at Wally's Groove World or at her place—she takes me on a trip down memory lane! She has a talent for describing everything so vividly: the sound, the venue, the crowd, the atmosphere, ... as if you were there with her.

When she invites me to her place, she cooks a delicious meal and we talk about life and music for hours. Besides sharing stories, musical knowledge and plenty of wisdom, I also know her as my plant mom. She is the one person I turn to for good practices and plant cuttings. The urban jungle at her apartment is almost as impressive as her music, books and objects cabinet.

JAN MACHIELS
Hill Men

After an internship at Clone records in Rotterdam in 2017, Koenie from Wally's Groove World offered me a position in his shop for a few days a week. It was there that I met Baby Bee and while packing hundreds of online orders and keeping the store open we got to know each other very well. Baby Bee is like an aunt to me. She has an incredible knowledge of music. I love to listen to her entertaining stories about the musical adventures she had with Smos in Café d'Anvers and Fuse and on gigs in Belgium, London or Paris.

SOME EPS SHE MADE ME DISCOVER AND THAT I STILL CARRY IN MY RECORD BAG:

Sun Electric—*O'Locco*
Kenny Larkin—*Loop 2*
Rhythm is Rhythm—*It Is What It Is*
Izmistik—*3rd Trace*
King Sunnt Adé and his African Beats—*Ja Funmi* (Remix)

BART VAN NESTE
Red D

My first memory of Smos & Baby Bee was at a party in Ghent's Vooruit in 1995. I do not remember which party, but I do remember they played the track *Sha-Dop* by Mystic Rythem on Peacefrog Records. I had just bought that record myself and loved it to bits.

It was rare for me to go out in Ghent around that time, because I was always hanging out at Fuse and other techno parties in Brussels and beyond. Around 1996 and 1997 I really started discovering and playing house music—realizing now that Sha-Dop is actually full-on house music—and started going out toin Silo and Café D'Anvers as well asnext to Fuse. Naturally I got to hear Smos & Baby Bee doing their thing. Every single time they were playing I heard at least one or two tracks I owned myself, so I was always happy when they were on the bill.

As a young DJ I enrolled in Diesel's U-Music talent contest. Smos and Baby Bee were in the jury, which encouraged me to play my A-game. To my great surprise I won. My own DJing started taking off around the end of the nineties and in the first part of the two thousands we started sharing the bill at various parties. I still strongly remember being booked to play at Café Capital where they were regulars, taking over from Smos after he played a Bobby Konders track I loved. I was still finding my ground as a DJ and after my set Smos told me that I played great records but he advised me to put them in a different order. To which I replied that he was not me, which made him roar with laughter at that newbie full of confidence.

In the years that followed we bumped into each other every now and then, especially when he was working in a sneaker shop near Ghent's Vooruit. When he was having a smoke outside and I passed by, we always had a nice chat. I do remember he was slowly coming to terms that nightlife and DJing were losing its appeal to him. To which I always replied that he would never be able to quit because DJing was in his blood.

Baby Bee was more the quiet and focused one in the background. When I visited Wally's Groove World where she was working in the back or when we met at parties or in record shops, we always had a nice chat. Most recently I got to spend a whole day at her place digging through hundreds of records and talking about life in general. It is a day that will always be engraved in my memory. Because truly, legends never die.

JACQUES DE MARSEILLE
Jacques Garotta

When you heard them play, you immediately understood what their musical culture was. I have a vivid memory of hearing Westbam's remix of Fad Gadget's *Collapsing New People*, for those who know. Their sets were very festive and eclectic. My first encounter with them must have been somewhere in the nineties, I think at Silo in Leuven. They were mostly known as DJs, like myself. We didn't thrive on our productions, we were investing all of our energy in the disc jockey craft.

I adore Belgium and its vibe, I'm probably the most Belgian of all French. Next to Holland and Spain, Belgium was the country I most frequented as a DJ in that era, up to 30 times a year. I was born and raised in Marseille but lived for a long time in Wattrelos near Lille and established a relationship with Belgian clubs and events such as Globe, Fuse, La Goa, *I Love Techno* or *Kozzmozz*, just to name a few. For some years I held a residency at Café d'Anvers. I often ran into Smos and Baby Bee. They were always smiling, I was always very pleased to meet them. My friendship with them is forever.

KOEN VAN IMMERSEEL
Koenie

In the early nineties I started DJing at Café d'Anvers, among others at the legendary Paradise parties hosted by Patrick Soks. I often played on Sunday nights. In love with the American garage and vocal house, we were able to push forward a distinctive sound, new and unheard at the time.

During one of those nights at Café d'Anvers I first met them, they were regulars. Later they began DJing in the club as well. They moved into the apartment above USA Import, the record shop where I worked at the time. When I started my own store dubbed Wally's Groove World in the basement of USA Import and focused on second hand records, Smos took my position and Baby Bee came working for me. Our lives were very connected.

BENOIT MEEUS

For about 10 years I was the official photographer at Café d'Anvers. As such, I joined their sound truck at the City Parade in Ghent in 2004 and was able to shoot some images of Smos and Baby Bee while DJing, surrounded by dancing crowds with the iconic rowing race course The Watersportbaan in the back. You see them playing vinyl records on a driving truck, which was quite adventurous given the sometimes bumpy ride. The images worked out really well with beautiful colors and a good composition. One was even used for the cover of nightlife magazine Move-X in June 2005.

Baby Bee on the cover of Belgian nightlife magazine Move-X (June 2005), photographed at the City Parade in Ghent in 2004. | © Benoit Meeus

BLOKSKES & MORE

Remarkable relics of the musical legacy of DJs and avid record collectors Smos & Baby Bee.

1 SWITCH - GET YA DUB ON (WHITE)
2 FREDERIC GALLIANO - WAKI RE-WORKS - F-COM WHITE
3 GOT YOUR WILD THING - SPIDERCUTS - WHITE
4 SILENT PARTNERS - DOWN BY DUB RMXS - HI PHEN PROMO
5 JAY TRIPWIRE - COVE REC 02 WHITE
6 FELIX RENNEFIELD - THE MAX - FUNKHAUS
7 TONY SENGHORE - FY FAN - OUTERGAZE WHITE
8 SWAYZAK - IN THE CARCRASH - K7
9 ISOLEE - IT'S ABOUT - FREUNDINNEN 01
10 STICKMAN 101 PROMO

April 2003

1 ROBERT DIETZ - PANDEMIC
2 STEREO EXPRESS - SHADOOBACK
3 NEGRU - KEEP ON
4 SAEED YOUNAN - KUMBALHA
5. CLASSIC
6. REDONDO - SIDEBURN
7. JOHNWAYNES - BELONG TO ME
8. ZAKES BANTWINI - WASTING MY TIME
9. HUGO GAMBO - DON'T STOP THE BEAT
10. LUCA LOZANO - THUG IT OUT
11. BLIND MINDED - TO THE BUS
12. WIGHNOMY BROTHERS - GUPPIPELTSCH
13. AFFKT - EL BALADRE
14. MAREK HEMMANN - GEMIN

1. Dead can dance: Spirit
2. System 7: Thunderdog
3. Chris & Cosey: The gates of ancient cities
4. T. Leary: Any reality is an opinion...
5. Dead can dance: Wilderness
6. J. Hassell/B. Eno: Rising thermal
7. D. Byrne/B. Eno: The carrier
8. O.M.D.: Time
9. Pink floyd: Julia
10. J. Hassell/B. Eno: Delta rain
11. Chris & Cosey: Baltjore
12. This mortal coil: Help me lift you up
13. Holger Czukay: Persian love
14. Deuter: Aum
15. Badrod cafe
16. System 7: Sunburst
17. D. Byrne: Red house

Sep. 1992

25/3/2002

Top 10 Smos and Baby Bee

1 - G&O, Post (Sunset recordings)
2 - Exelar meets Garcynoise, Tonight this (D.Press industries)
3 - Hécher & Ward , Cosmic vibes e.p.(Tweekin)
4 - Tiefschwarz, Acid soul (Classic)
5 - Harry Morse project, I'm on fire (Big wave)
6 - The rapture, House of jealous lovers (DFA)
7 - Jay-J, Of your body (Loveslap)
8 - Akufen, Psychometry vol.3 (Trapez)
9 - Organic dub series vol. 2 (Frozen)
10 - Duncan, Fantasia (Yellow)

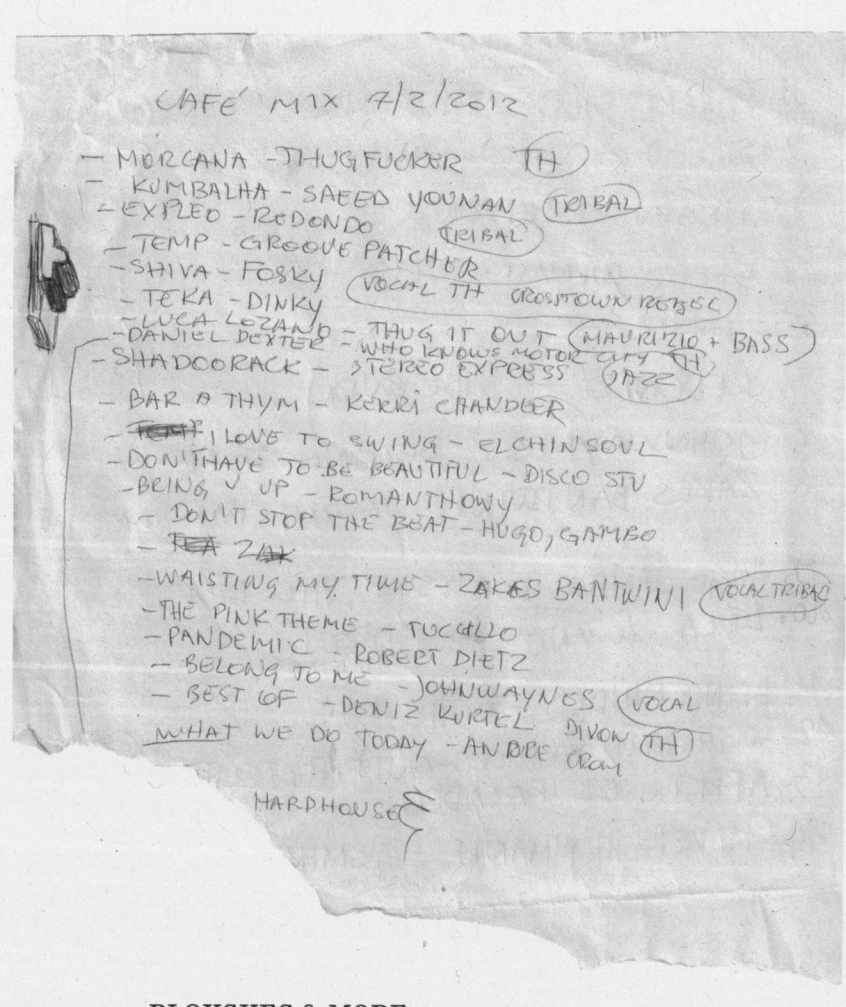

CAFÉ MIX 7/2/2012

- MORCANA - THUGFUCKER (TH)
- KUMBALHA - SAEED YOUNAN (TRIBAL)
- EXPLEO - REDONDO (TRIBAL)
- TEMP - GROOVE PATCHER
- SHIVA - FOSKY (VOCAL TH CROSSTOWN REBEL)
- TEKA - DINKY
- LUCA LOZANO - THUG IT OUT (MAURIZIO + BASS)
- DANIEL DEXTER - WHO KNOWS MOTOR CITY TH
- SHADOORACK - STEREO EXPRESS (JAZZ)
- BAR A THYM - KERRI CHANDLER
- I LOVE TO SWING - ELCHINSOUL
- DON'T HAVE TO BE BEAUTIFUL - DISCO STU
- BRING ∨ UP - ROMANTHONY
- DON'T STOP THE BEAT - HUGO, GAMBO
- ZAK
- WAISTING MY TIME - ZAKES BANTWINI (VOCAL TRIBAL)
- THE PINK THEME - TUCCILLO
- PANDEMIC - ROBERT DIETZ
- BELONG TO ME - JOHNWAYNES (VOCAL)
- BEST OF - DENIZ KURTEL DIVON (TH)
- WHAT WE DO TODAY - ANDRE CROM

HARDHOUSE

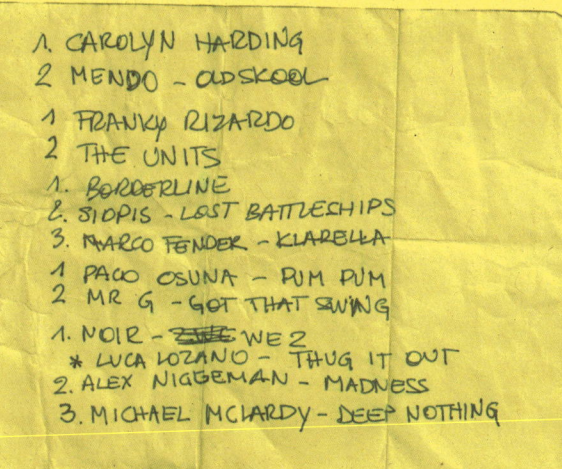

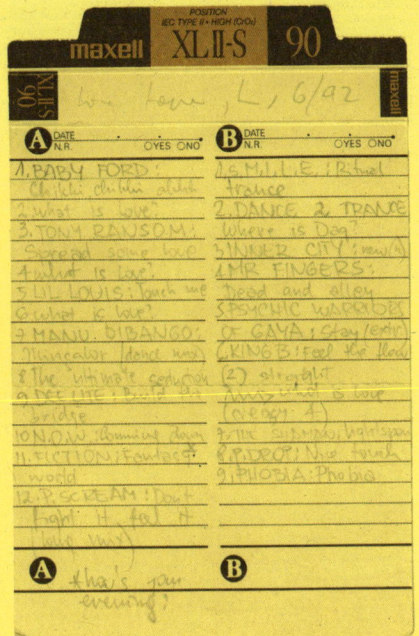

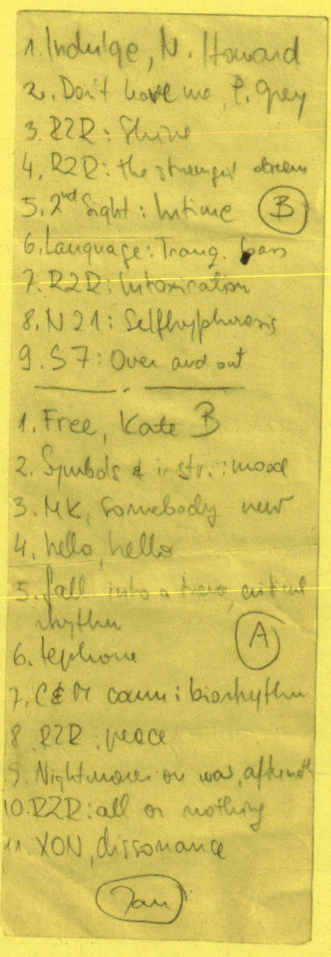

CD 1   20 YEARS

1. DNH - EROTIC ILLUSION
2. HERMANN - TUMBLIN' DOWN - MK DUB
3. WAYNE ROLLINS - BC'S PIMP THEME
4. CLUB ORCHESTRA - THRILLSEEKERS DUB
5. RALPHIE ROSARIO - DA-ME-LO
6. PIZARRO - SUELTA ME
7. BUNGIE - PHREAK BEAT
8. SIR DANE - BOP TILL YOU DROP
9. HARDTRAXX - NEEDFULL THINGS
10. ALLEN STREET - THINKING BOUT YOUR LOVE
11. 3 GUYS ON WARWICK - ADICTED
12. GOLDFINGER - I COULD LEARN

CD 2.   20 YEARS

1. SOUL PARTY 1992 VOCODED
2. SOUL PARTY VOCODED DUBBIER
3. SOUL PARTY - BACK INTO TIME !
4. WANT YOUR GROOVE - LOVE IS THE MESSAGE
5. EARTH PEOPLE - DANCE
6. DEEP COLLECTIVE - KEEP IT OPEN
7. DJ SHON - REJOICE
8. ROOTS + WINGS - COME OVER TO MY PLACE
9. RICKY ROUGE - STRANGE LOVE
10. TODD TERRY - PUT YOUR HANDS TOGETHER
11. TODD TERRY - WHEN YOU HOLD ME
12. WEEKEND - SATURDAY & SUNDAY

BABY BEE Special

Dear Smos&B., just because I keep on talking about that one cassette you made me ; Here is a copy of my most pecious "Baby Bee Special".
(I know it's a bit like bringing water to the sea, but anyway.)
I admire your musical ears, brains and soul that makes rhythms a continues joy !! xxx Bruno

COMPILATIONS

Smos & Baby Bee were invited as curators of compilation CD albums on three different occassions. For a long time and prior to the domination of digital streaming services and free online DJ mixes on platforms such as Soundcloud or Mixcloud, the mixed compilation CD was a popular and chart-topping concept. Unlike its modern variant, these albums were long in the making: a provisional tracklisting was made; permissions were requested from record companies and/or artists; the DJ mix was recorded and (sometimes) re-recorded, until perfection was reached.

25 Years Paradise
541, CD, 2016

1. Night Communication — *Lose Control* (In Dub We Trust Mix)
2. Kevin Saunderson feat. Inner City — *Ahnonghay* (Original Reese Mix)
3. Robert Owens — *I'll Be Your Friend* (Original DEF mix)
4. Mr. Marvin — *Hammond Groove*
5. Freaks — *Dance & Disorder* (From The Wax Mix Without Acid)
6. Derrick L. Carter — *Dreaming Again*
7. Koenie & Frederik — *Storm*
8. Nu-World — *Chrystol Dance* (Tiny Tom Mix)
9. KC Flightt — *Let's Get Jazzy* (Dope Mix)
10. The D.O.C. — *Portrait Of A Masterpiece* (Hip Hop 12" Extended)
11. Mike Wilson feat. Shawn Christopher — *Another Sleepless Night* (Redzone Mix)
12. Omniverse — *Antares*
13. Virgo Four — *In A Vision*
14. Psychotropic — *Only For The Headstrong*
15. That Kid Chris — *Keep On (Pressin' On)* (Rhythmix)
16. Optik — *The Chance* (Remix)
17. Kevin Saunderson Pres. The Reese Project — *I Believe* (Carl Craig B-Dub Mix)

Cafe D'Anvers (10 Years)
Current & Past Tunes
(Discomatic, CD, 2000)

CD2 *Past Tunes*
1. The Underground Solution—*Luv Dancin* (Egotrip Mix)
2. Don Carlos—*Alone* (Flute House Mix)
3. Funky Green Dogs From Outer Space—*Reach For Me* (Vibe Mix)
4. First Choice—*Armed And Extremely Dangerous* (DJ D's Dub Science Mix)
5. Alex Neri—*Planet Funk* (Planet Funk Club Mix)
6. DJ Toys Vol. 1—*Tech Disco Excerpts* (Never Let You Go Mix)
7. DJ Spen Presents Jasper Street Company—*A Feeling'* (Paradox Vocal Mix)
8. Marcel Krieg—*Take A Ride II* (Percussion Mix)
9. Q-Burns Abstract Message—*Mess Of Afros* (Glenn Underground Remix)
10. Raw—*Shit Goddamn* (Shit Goddamn Mix)
11. Green Flame & MRG—*Back From The T* (Part 1)
12. The Juggernaut Express—*Pizza Panic* (Pizza Panic Mix)
13. Cliff De L'Isle & Eric Cycle—*Fly Me* (Eric's Sunny Side Mix)
14. Freaks—*The Shrunken Head* (The Beat Freak Mix)
15. Tribal Liberation—*Warrior Drums*
16. Kama Sutra—*Night Walk* (Black Horses Mix)

Cafe D'Anvers Presents
Free Vibes & Saturdays
(Discomatic, CD, 2001)

1. Jay-J & Macari—*El Vagabundo*
2. Pound Boys vs. Martello Bros.—*Jack It Up* (Johnny Corporate Dub)
3. DJ Prinz—*My Sound* (The Dealer)
4. Souldoubt—*Midtown* (This Is The Place)
5. Guiro—*Free* (Sounds Of Life Dub)
6. Kidstuff—*Love It*
7. Julien Jabre—*Voodance*
8. Inner City—*Good Love* (Joey Negro Radar Dub)
9. DJ Prinz—*Jazz* (Original Mix)
10. DJ F.E.X—*I Feel U* (DJ F.E.X Mix)
11. Yann Fontaine—*Can You Feel It* (Marius Remix)
12. Groove Cartel—*Ultralove* (Llorca's Ultrasax Remix)

1. Blake—*Saturday Night* (Deep Dub Mix)
2. Mayaku—*Mayaku's Theme* (Late Night Mix)
3. Trevor Loveys—*My Land* (Original Mix)
4. Barada—*Robo* (Porn Mix)
5. Silver Haze—*Every Day*
6. Kemu—*Park Shiner*
7. Michel De Hey vs. Grooveyard—*Compound*
8. Inland Knights—*Creative Spaces* (Up The Wall Mix)
9. Shur-i-kan—*Cookie* (Discerning Era Bang-I-Can Remix)
10. Tiefschwarz—*On Up*
11. Freaks—*Dance & Disorder* (From The Wax–Without Acid Remix)
12. Ernest Saint Laurent—*Clumsy Lobster* (Harvey's Weekender Mix)

FLYER ARCHIVE

Friday 30. 04. 1993, *Acid Test*
at Café d'Anvers, Antwerp, 100 × 150 mm.

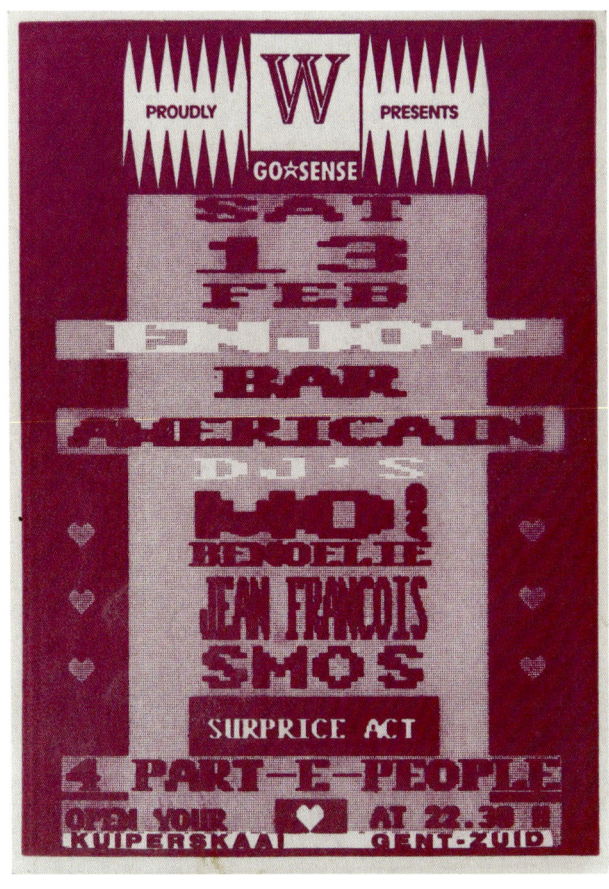

Saturday 13. 02. 1993,
Bar Americain, Ghent, 115 × 160 mm.

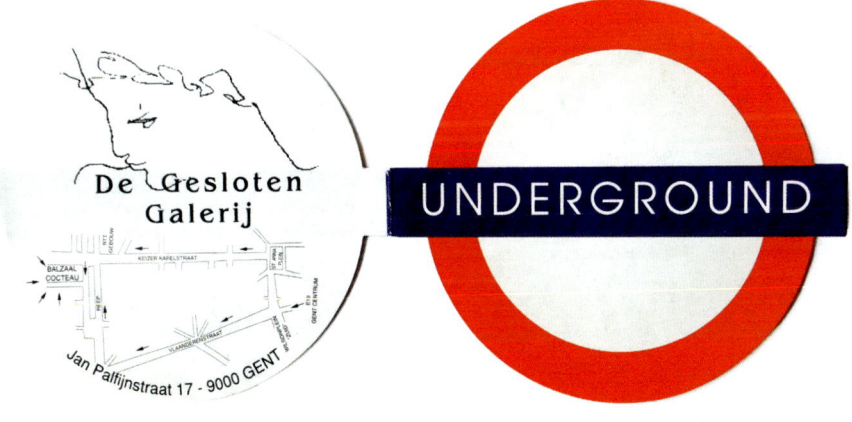

Saturday 06. 11. 1993, *Alice In Wonderland*
at Cocteau, Ghent, 270 × 120 mm.

Monday 22. 11. 1993, *Magical Musical
Morsels* at Le Vaudeville, Brussels, 105 × 75 mm.

April 1993, Le Vaudeville,
Brussels, 210 × 105 mm.

Saturday 13. 02. 1993,
Bar Americain, Ghent, 115 × 160 mm.

Saturday 06. 11. 1993, *Alice In Wonderland*
at Cocteau, Ghent, 270 × 120 mm.

April 1993, Le Vaudeville, Brussels,
210 × 105 mm.

Monday 22. 11. 1993, *Magical Musical Morsels*
at Le Vaudeville, Brussels, 105 × 75 mm.

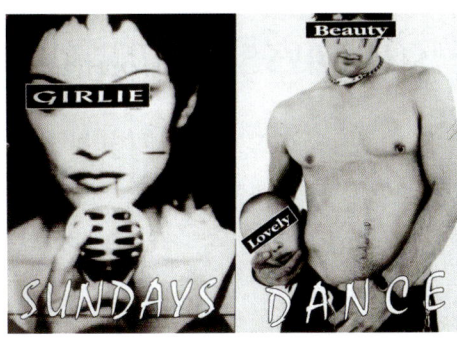
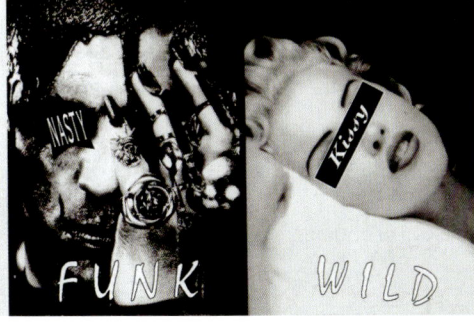

Thursday 11. 11. 1993, *Sundays* at Le Disque Rouge, Brussels, 300 × 100 mm.

December 1993, *New Year* at La Demence, Brussels, 250 × 125 mm.

Wednesday 10. 11. 1993, *Barbarella* at Selekest, Ghent, 245 × 90 mm.

Saturday 02. 10. 1993, *Kastanjebal / Bal des Marrons* at Cocteau, Ghent, 210 × 95 mm.

17.–27. 07. 1993, *Gentse Feesten* at Cafee Zodiac, Ghent, 210 × 140 mm.

JAN WELVAERT
&
MARNIX CATACOMBES
present on

10th NOVEMBER

THE BEST SHOW
AND PARTY OF
THE YEAR

at SELEKEST – St Salvatorstraat 38 –
9000 GENT – TEL 09/ 224 22 48

D.J. JOHNSON
U.K.
MASTERMIX DJ
HAVANA AMSTERDAM

D.J. SMOS
CATACOMBES
ZODIAC

D.J. BABY BEE
THE JAN WELVAERT PARTIES

D.J. QUINTEN
CATACOMBES

SURPRISES & FASHION
ACTS

PLEASE GO AS
BARBARELLA MAD

DOORS OPEN AT 22.00 HOURS
BE EARLY

Wednesday 10. 11. 1993, *Barbarella*
at Selekest, Ghent, 245 × 90 mm.

"SUNDAYS"
A NEW VENUE
FOR
TOP MODELS - DRAG QUEENS -
LOLITAS - BEAUTIFUL STUDS -
QUEERS - FASHION VICTIMS -
CELEBRITIES - OLIVIAS & MARINAS
GROUPIES -
SHINY HAPPY PEOPLE -
AND OF COURSE :
YOU !

"SUNDAYS"
with

MUSIC : JON DASILVA
(Manchester - UK)
SMOS & BABY B.
FRANK (Zodiac-Ghent)

GOGO'S : BURNING
PUSSY POWER

DOOR POLICY : JUNIOR
&
SECURITY BODY GUARDS

Jan Bizar

"SUNDAYS"
IS
A MIXED DANCE
EVENT
(GIRLS ARE MORE THAN WELCOME)
BY
JAN BIZAR
AT
LE DISQUE ROUGE
Rue Blaes 208
1000 Brussels

"SUNDAYS"
START
NOVEMBER 28TH
11 PM

ENTRANCE
300 BF

NEXT PARTY :
DECEMBER 26th

Thursday 11. 11. 1993, *Sundays* at Le Disque
Rouge, Brussels, 300 × 100 mm.

December 1993, *New Year*
at La Demence, Brussels, 250 × 125 mm.

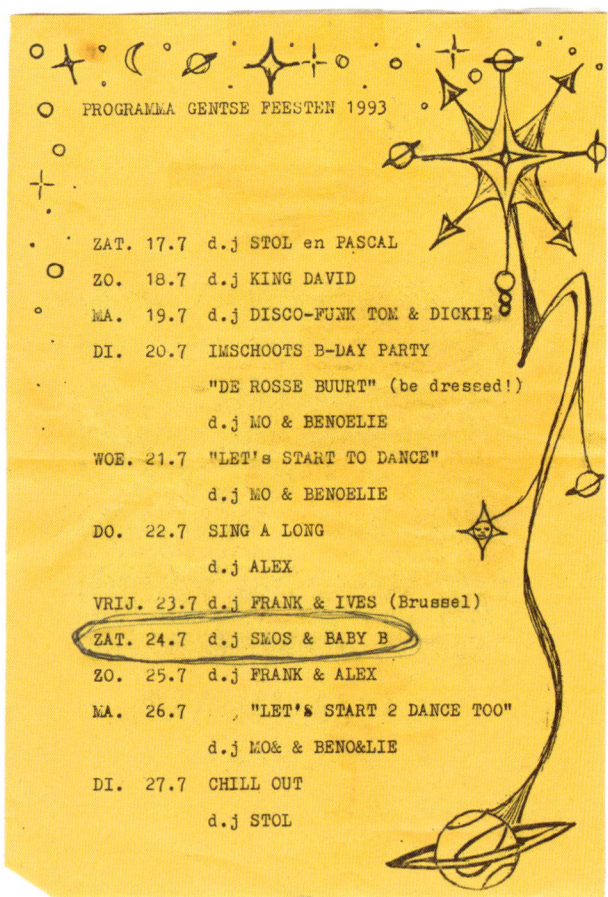

17.–27. 07. 1993, *Gentse Feesten* at Cafee Zodiac,
Ghent, 210 × 140 mm.

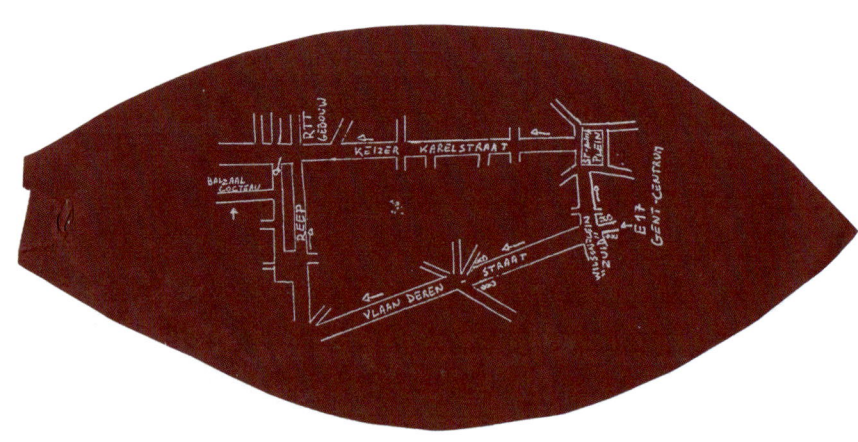

Saturday 02. 10. 1993, *Kastanjebal /
Bal des Marrons* at Cocteau, Ghent, 210 × 95 mm.

← February & March 1994, *Flight* at Le Vaudeville, Brussels, 215 × 110 mm.

↓ Sunday 11. 09. 1994, *Sundays* at Rue Blaesstraat 208, Brussels, 150 × 105 mm.

↓↓ Sunday 23. 10. 1994, *Sundays* at Rue Blaesstraat 208, Brussels, 150 × 100 mm.

↓↓↓ Sunday 10. 04. 1994, *Sundays* at Le Disque Rouge, Brussels, 150 × 105 mm.

November 1994, Café d'Anvers, Antwerp, 145 × 155 mm.

Saturday 05. 02. 1994, *Love* at Chic, Ghent, 105 × 150 mm.

February & March 1994, *Flight* at Le Vaudeville, Brussels, 215 × 110 mm.

Sunday 10. 04. 1994, *Sundays* at Le Disque Rouge, Brussels, 150 × 105 mm.

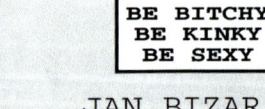

Sunday 23. 10. 1994, *Sundays* at Rue Blaesstraat 208, Brussels, 150 × 100 mm.

Sunday 11. 09. 1994, *Sundays* at Rue Blaesstraat 208, Brussels, 150 × 105 mm.

Saturday 05. 02. 1994, *Love* at Chic, Ghent, 105 × 150 mm.

Sunday 01. 05. 1994, *Soul Food Inc. presents Phuture* at Le Palais, Antwerp, 170 × 110 mm.

December 1994, *20 Years USA Import*, Antwerp, 210 × 150 mm.

Sunday 06. 11. 1994, *Essential Elements Party* at Café d'Anvers, Antwerp, 150 × 105 mm.

1994, *Unity Power*, Le Drouot, Brussels, 2100 × 950 mm.

December 1994, *20 Years USA Import*, Antwerp, 210 × 150 mm.

Sunday 01. 05. 1994, *Soul Food Inc. presents Phuture* at Le Palais, Antwerp, 170 × 110 mm.

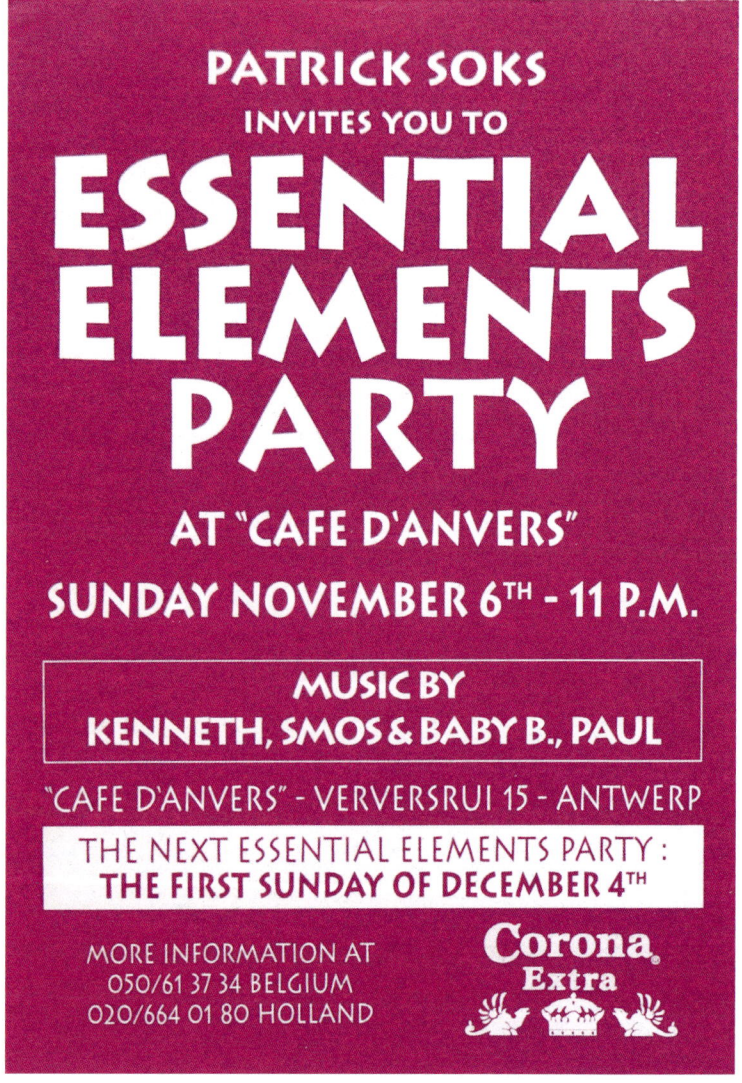

Sunday 06. 11. 1994, *Essential Elements Party* at Café d'Anvers, Antwerp, 150 × 105 mm.

October 1995, *James Bond in Paradise* at Café d'Anvers, Antwerp, 300 × 155 mm.

Sunday 20. 08. 1995, *Cyber Space Trip 1* at Silo, Leuven, 190 × 125 mm.

Friday 02. 06. 1995, *Who's Who's Follies* at Fuse / La Demence, Brussels, 220 × 150 mm.

Thursday 16. 02. 1995, *Keystone Défilé* at Café d'Anvers, Antwerp, 155 × 105 mm.

March & April 1995, Lido Club, Leuven, 205 × 150 mm.

1995

October 1995, *James Bond in Paradise* at Café d'Anvers, Antwerp, 300 × 155 mm.

Sunday 20. 08. 1995, *Cyber Space Trip 1* at Silo, Leuven, 190 × 125 mm.

Friday 02. 06. 1995, *Who's Who's Follies* at Fuse / La Demence, Brussels, 220 × 150 mm.

March & April 1995, Lido Club, Leuven, 205 × 150 mm.

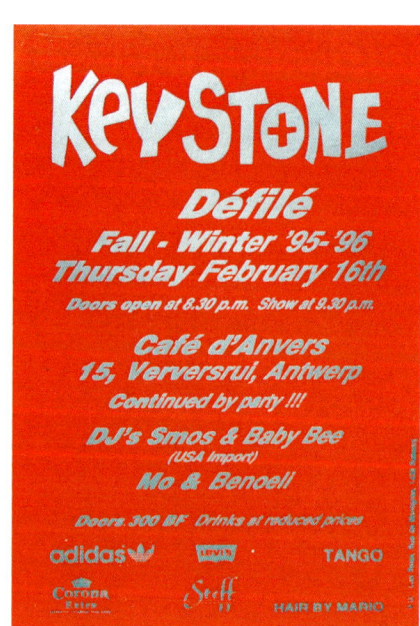

Thursday 16. 02. 1995, *Keystone Défilé* at Café d'Anvers, Antwerp, 155 × 105 mm.

Monday 25. 12. 1995, *Christmas in Paradise* at Café d'Anvers, Antwerp, 210 × 150 mm.

Friday 03. 02. 1995, *Disco Fever* at D-Light, Brussels, 150 × 100 mm.

March 1995, Fuse, Brussels, 210 × 150 mm.

Monday 25. 12. 1995, *Christmas in Paradise* at Café d'Anvers, Antwerp, 210 × 150 mm.

Friday 03. 02. 1995, *Disco Fever* at D-Light, Brussels, 150 × 100 mm.

March 1995, Fuse, Brussels, 210 × 150 mm.

46   1995

Friday 15. 11. 1996, *Lick Da Future* at Café d'Anvers, Antwerp, 210 × 150 mm.

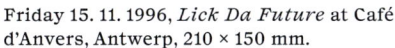

Thursday 28. 03. 1996, *xpansions of the mind* at Pacific, Antwerp, 185 × 125 mm.

Friday 28. 06. 1996, *Marvelously Mellow* at Southside, Antwerp, 105 × 70 mm.

November & December 1996, *Who's Who's Land*, Brussels, 150 × 105 mm.

Sunday 10. 11. 1996, *ooops... wrong planet* at Café d'Anvers, Antwerp, ⌀ 170 mm.

1996

Friday 28. 06. 1996, *Marvelously Mellow* at Southside, Antwerp, 105 × 70 mm.

Friday 15. 11. 1996, *Lick Da Future* at Café d'Anvers, Antwerp, 210 × 150 mm.

Thursday 28. 03. 1996, *xpansions of the mind* at Pacific, Antwerp, 185 × 125 mm.

Sunday 10. 11. 1996, *ooops... wrong planet* at Café d'Anvers, Antwerp, ⌀ 170 mm.

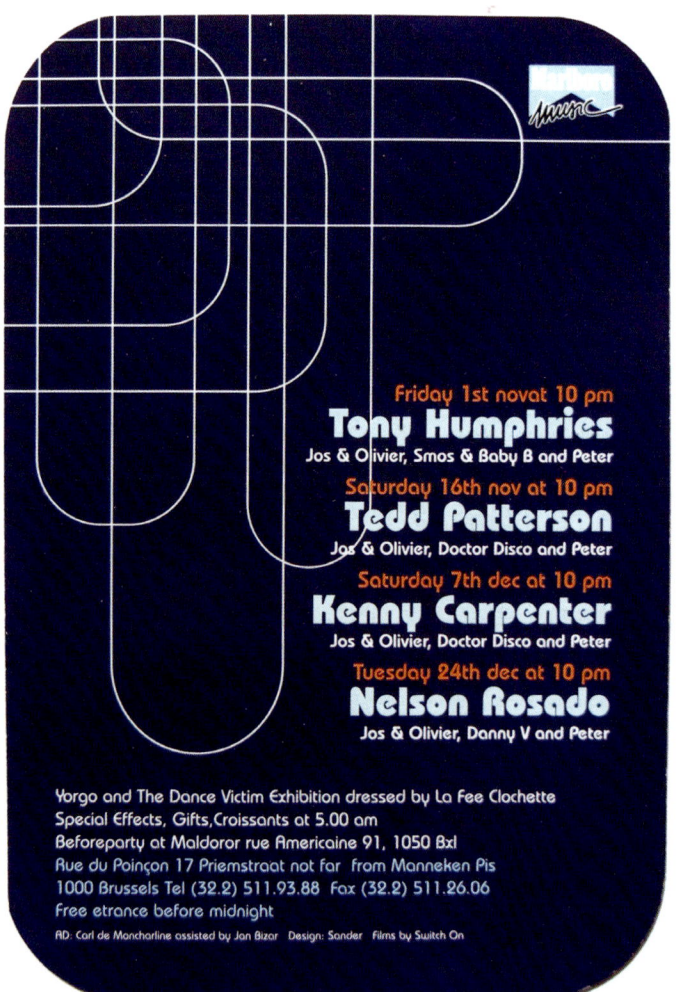

November & December 1996, *Who's Who's Land*, Brussels, 150 × 105 mm.

Friday 22. 11. 1996, *Equinox Futur*
at Café d'Anvers, Antwerp, 160 × 105 mm.

December 1996,
nu'skool at Café d'Anvers,
Antwerp, ⌀170.

Tuesday 24. 12. 1996, *Paradise*
at Café d'Anvers, Antwerp, 175 × 120 mm.

Friday 16. 02. 1996,
Love D'Ohm at Silo,
Leuven, 120 × 110 mm.

Thursday 31. 10. 1996, *Paradise*
at Café d'Anvers, Antwerp, 175 × 120 mm.

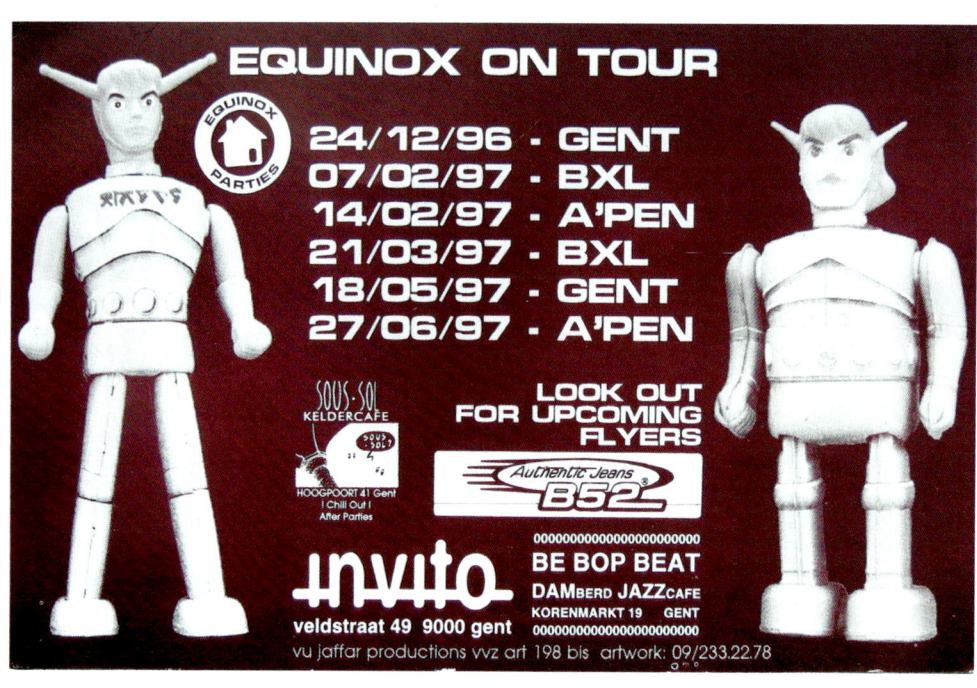

Friday 22. 11. 1996, *Equinox Futur*
at Café d'Anvers, Antwerp, 160 × 105 mm.

Tuesday 24. 12. 1996, *Paradise*
at Café d'Anvers, Antwerp, 175 × 120 mm.

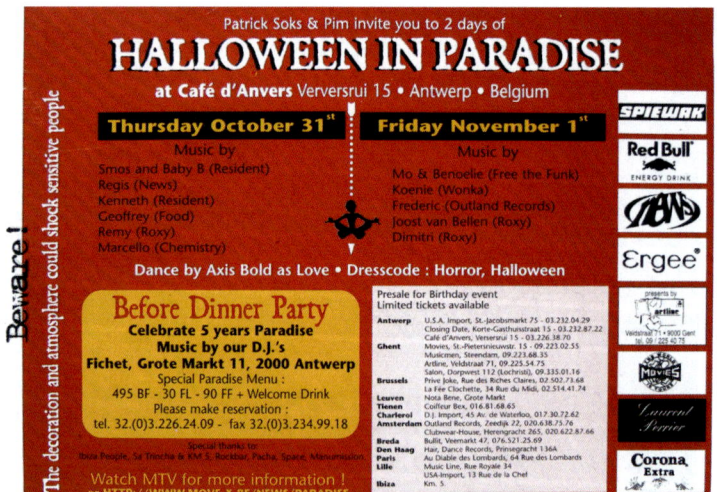

Thursday 31. 10. 1996, *Paradise*
at Café d'Anvers, Antwerp, 175 × 120 mm.

Friday 16. 02. 1996,
Love D'Ohm at Silo,
Leuven, 120 × 110 mm.

July 1996, 10 days of techno, Ghent, 310 × 150 mm.

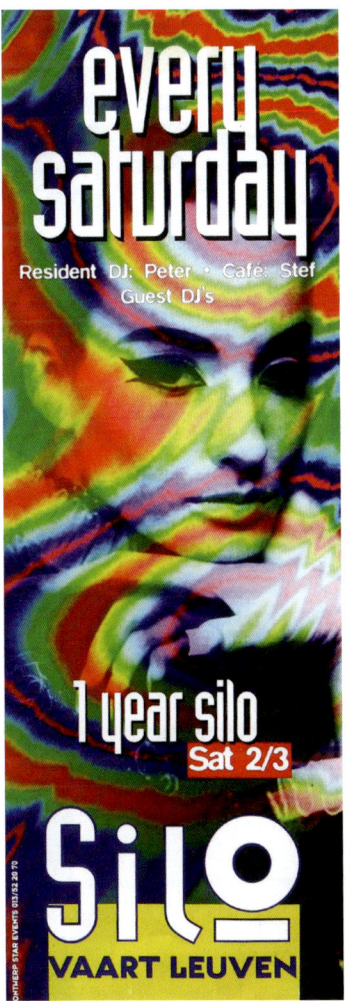

February 1996, Silo, Leuven, 300 × 105 mm.

Les soirées stars at Le Star, Ghent, 310 × 150 mm.

Thursday 30. 10. 1997, *L'Enfer d'Anvers*
at Zillion, Antwerp, 220 × 73 mm.

Saturday 08. 11. 1997, *Clock Work Orange Party*
at Atmozphere, Zottegem, 120 × 120 mm.

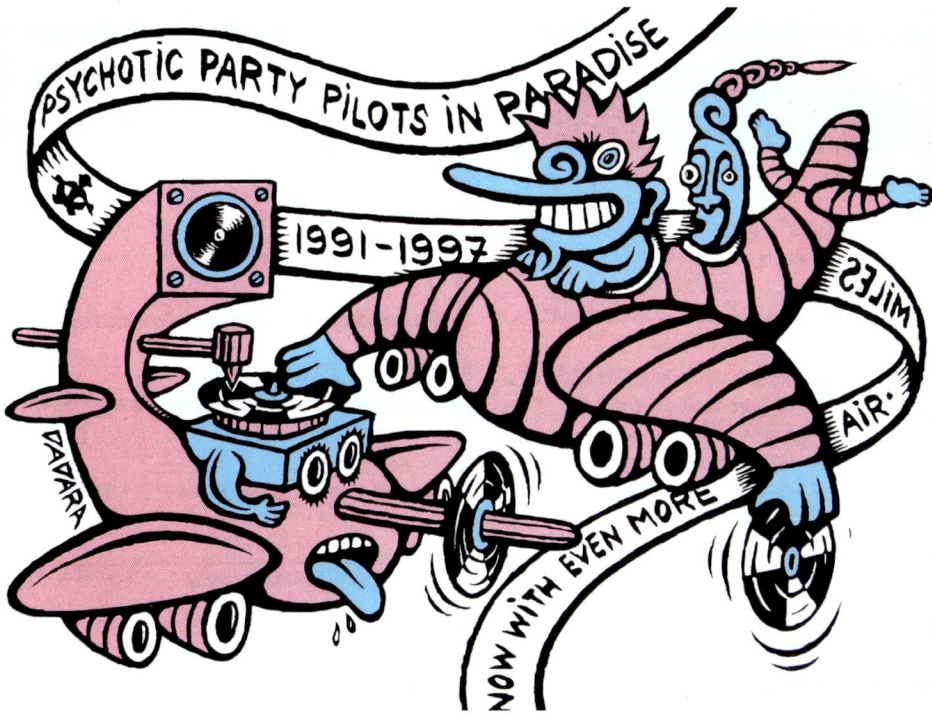

Friday 31. 10. 1997, *Paradise*
at Café d'Anvers, Antwerp, 175 × 120 mm.

Saturday 25. 10. 1997, *Cruises To Pleasure*
at Bateau Roulette, Antwerp, 230 × 145 mm.

Friday 28. 03. 1997, *Magic Life* at Fuse,
Brussels, 110 × 110 mm.

Thursday 30. 10. 1997, *L'Enfer d'Anvers*
at Zillion, Antwerp, 220 × 73 mm.

Saturday 08. 11. 1997, *Clock Work Orange Party*
at Atmozphere, Zottegem, 120 × 120 mm.

Friday 31. 10. 1997, *Paradise*
at Café d'Anvers, Antwerp, 175 × 120 mm.

Friday 28. 03. 1997, *Magic Life* at Fuse,
Brussels, 110 × 110 mm.

Saturday 25. 10. 1997, *Cruises To Pleasure*
at Bateau Roulette, Antwerp, 230 × 145 mm.

November 1997, The Hall, Liège,
210 × 150 mm.

Friday 07. 02. 1997, The House Of Disco at Fuse,
Brussels, 150 × 105 mm.

Sunday 14. 09. 1997, *Deep Rain Forest Party*
at Private Swing Café, Knokke, 295 × 150 mm.

Sunday 09. 11. 1997, *Andy Psychonight*
at tour de l'est, Antwerp, 325 × 70 mm.

Friday 14. 02. 1997, *The House Of Love* at Café d'Anvers, Antwerp, 150 × 105 mm.

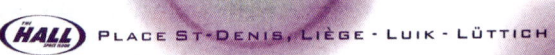

November 1997, The Hall, Liège, 210 × 150 mm.

Sunday 14. 09. 1997, *Deep Rain Forest Party* at Private Swing Café, Knokke, 295 × 150 mm.

Sunday 09. 11. 1997, *Andy Psychonight* at tour de l'est, Antwerp, 325 × 70 mm.

Friday 19. 12. 1997, *Tunes From Da House* at Myles Ballroom, Kontich, 145 × 95 mm.

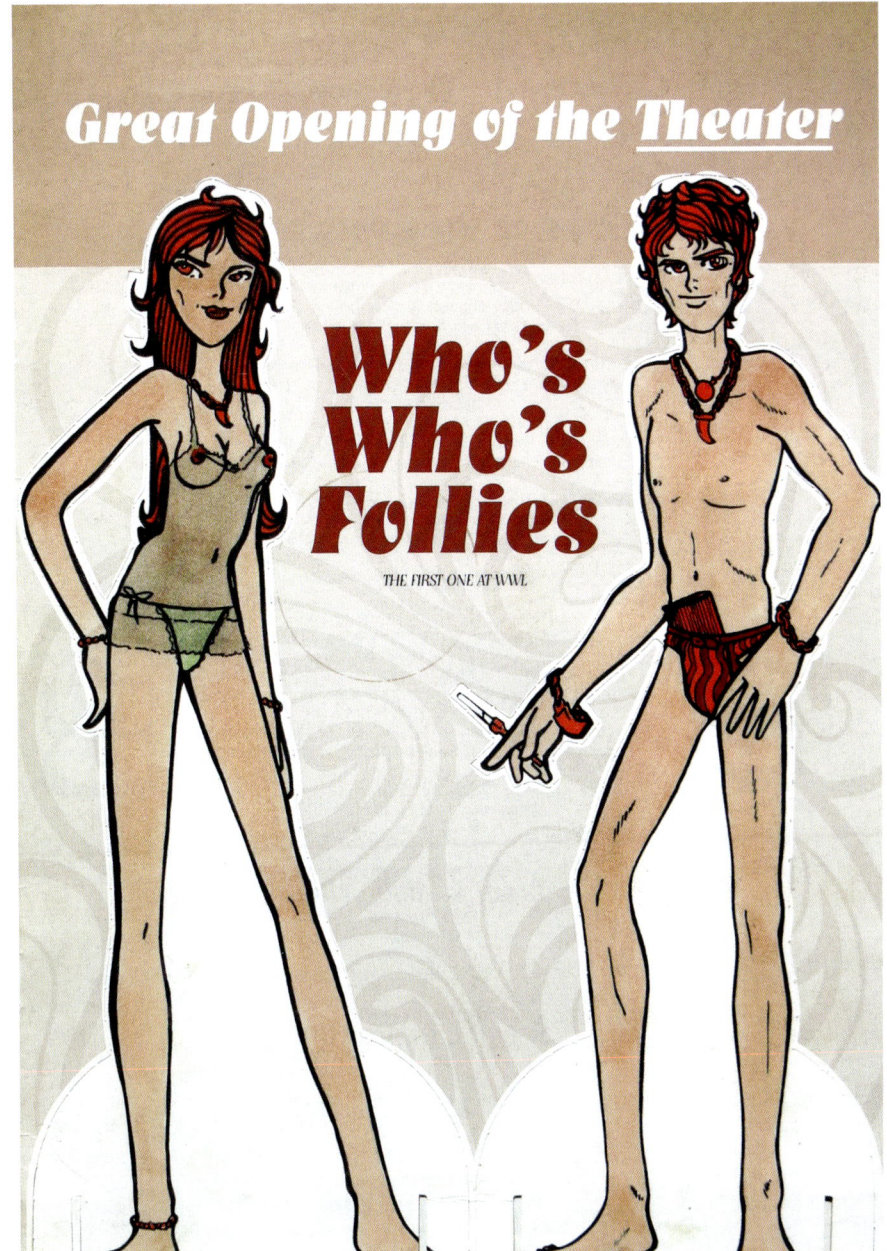

Saturday 28. 06. 1997, *Who's Who's Land*, Brussels, 300 × 210 mm.

Wednesday 31. 12. 1997, *Who's Who's Land*, Brussels, 100 × 100 mm.

1997

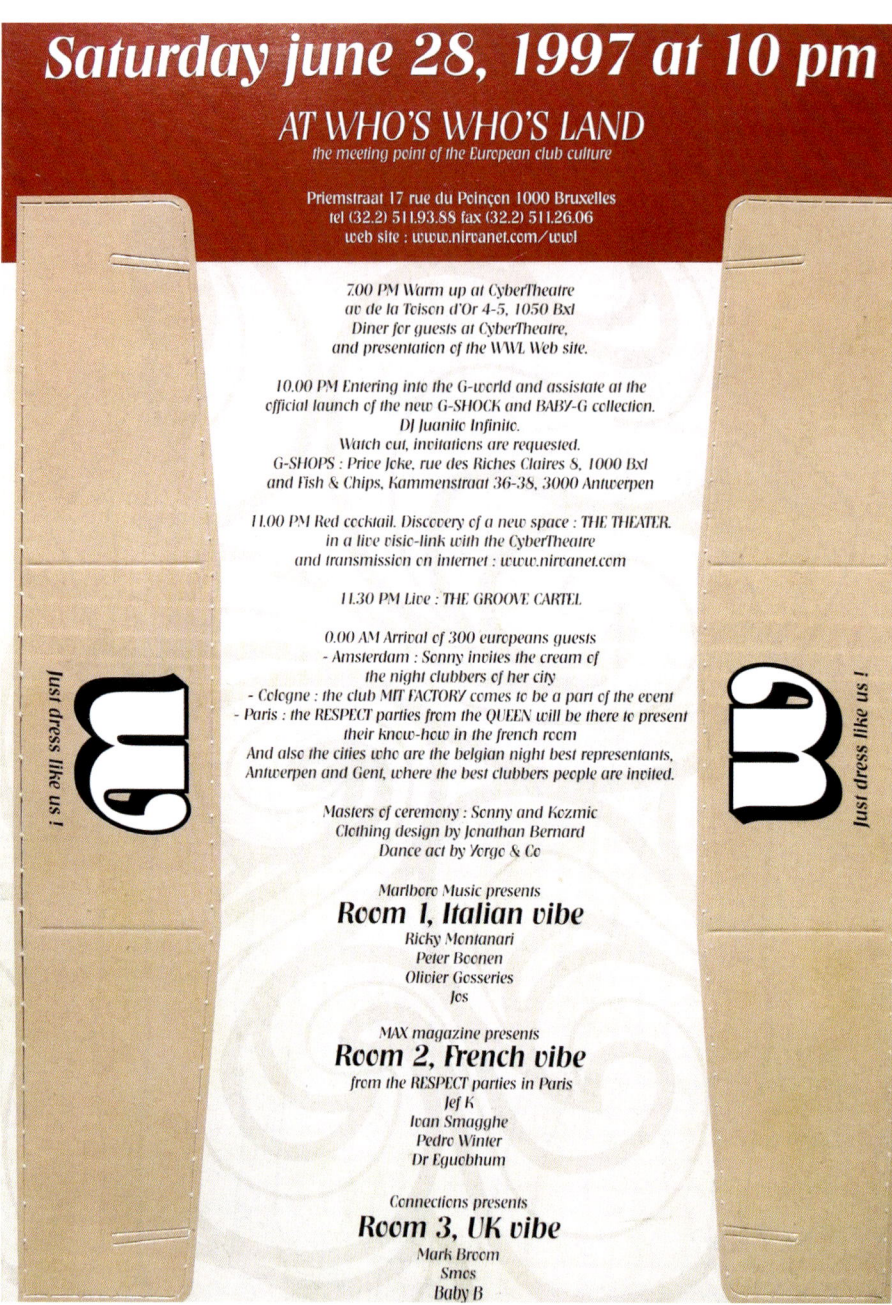

Saturday 28. 06. 1997, *Who's Who's Land*, Brussels, 300 × 210 mm.

Friday 19. 12. 1997, *Tunes From Da House* at Myles Ballroom, Kontich, 145 × 95 mm.

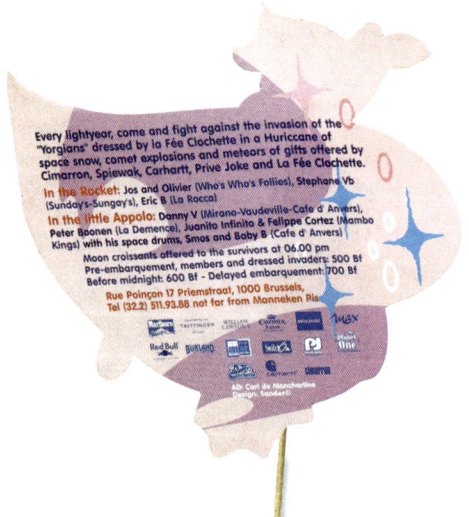

Wednesday 31. 12. 1997, *Who's Who's Land*, Brussels, 100 × 100 mm.

Thursday 31. 12. 1998, *1999*
at Eskimo Factory, Ghent, 145 × 200 mm.

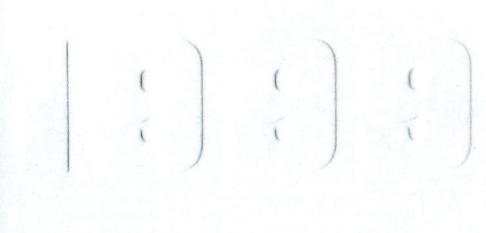

October 1998, *Le Rêve d'O*,
Tournai, 295 × 103 mm.

Saturday 19. 09. 1998, *Barclay Catwalk*
at Slaughterhouse , Antwerp, 800 × 400 mm.

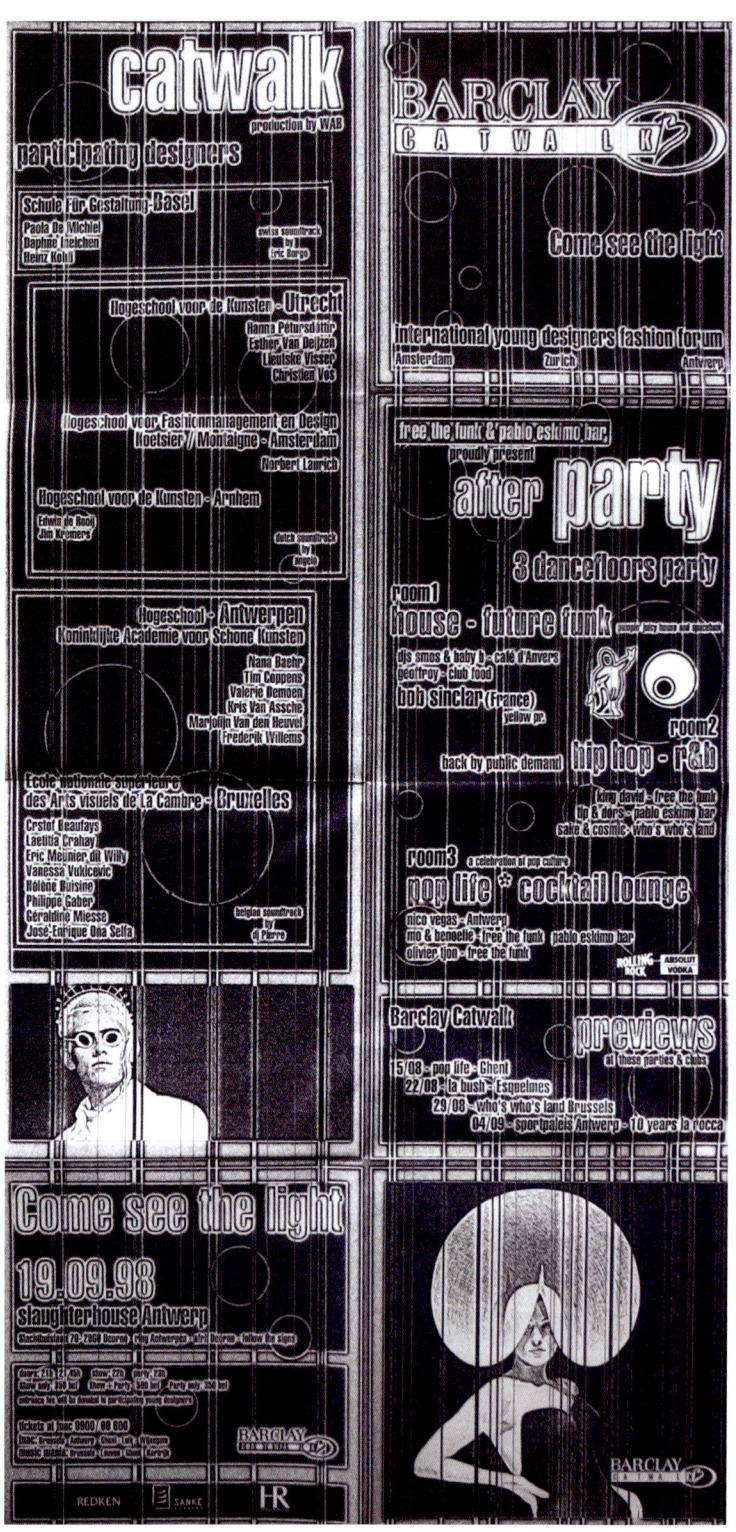

Saturday 19. 09. 1998, *Barclay Catwalk*
at Slaughterhouse, Antwerp, 800 × 400 mm.

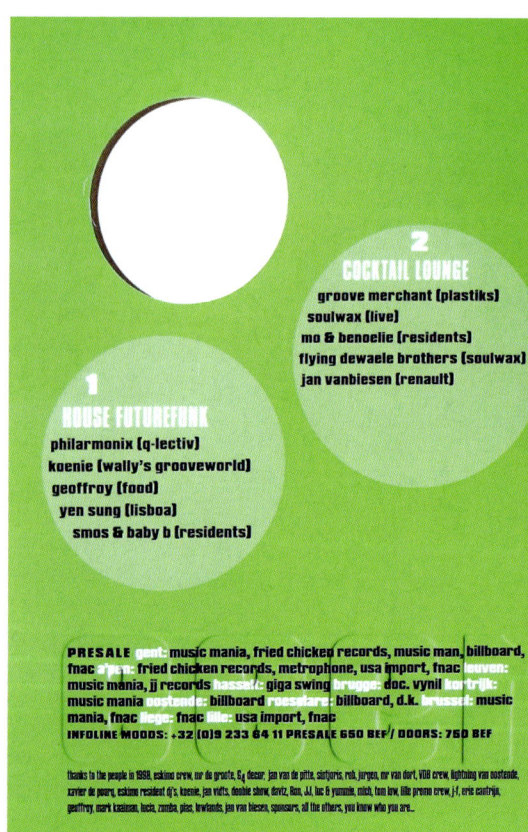

Thursday 31. 12. 1998, *1999*
at Eskimo Factory, Ghent, 145 × 200 mm.

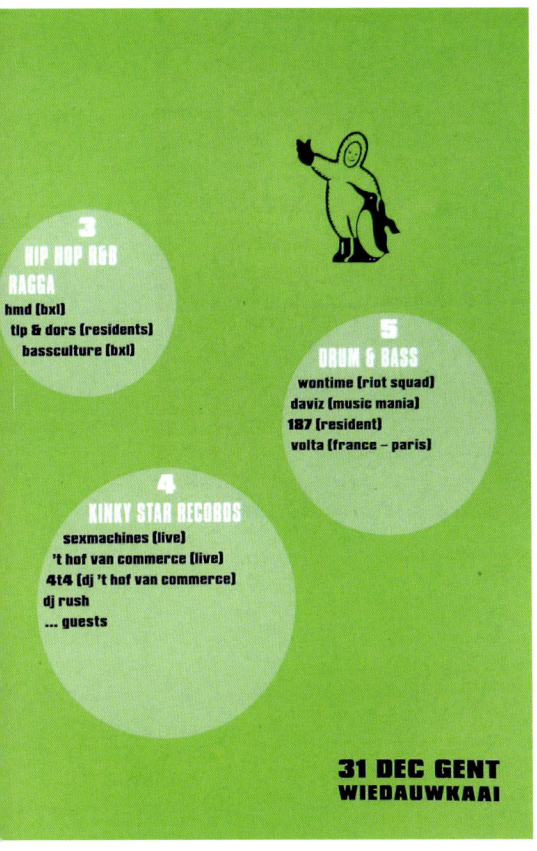

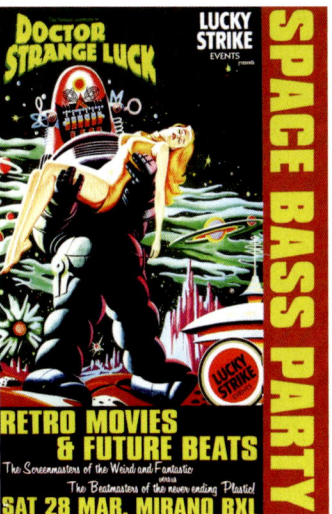

Saturday 28. 03. 1998, *Doctor Strangeluck* at Mirano, Brussels, 190 × 150 mm.

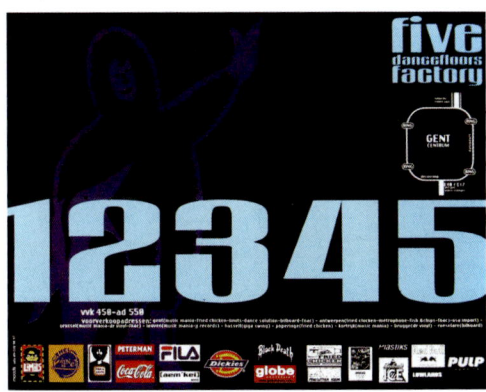

Saturday 25. 04. 1998, *5 Dancefloors Factory* at Pablo Eskimo Bar, Ghent, 195 × 150 mm.

Thursday 31. 12. 1998, Café d'Anvers, Antwerp, 420 × 145 mm.

October 1998, *Le Rêve d'O*, Tournai, 295 × 103 mm.

Sunday 26. 04. 1998, Food, Leuven, 150 × 150 mm.

Thursday 31. 12. 1998,
Café d'Anvers, Antwerp, 420 × 145 mm.

Saturday 28. 03. 1998, *Doctor Strangeluck*
at Mirano, Brussels, 190 × 150 mm

Saturday 25. 04. 1998, *5 Dancefloors Factory*
at Pablo Eskimo Bar, Ghent, 195 × 150 mm.

Sunday 26. 04. 1998, Food,
Leuven, 150 × 150 mm.

December 1998, *Mixomatose* at Café d'Anvers and Decadance, Antwerp, Ghent, 300 × 70 mm.

Saturday 07. 11. 1998, *Eskimo* at Eskimo Factory, Ghent, 195 × 150 mm.

Friday 10. 04. 1998, *Pussy Galore*, Brussels, 160 × 160 mm.

Saturday 21. 03. 1998, *Super 45 Tours* at Catacombes, Roeselare, 174 × 174 mm.

Thursday 30. 04. 1998, *H₂0*, Pecq, 200 × 100 mm.

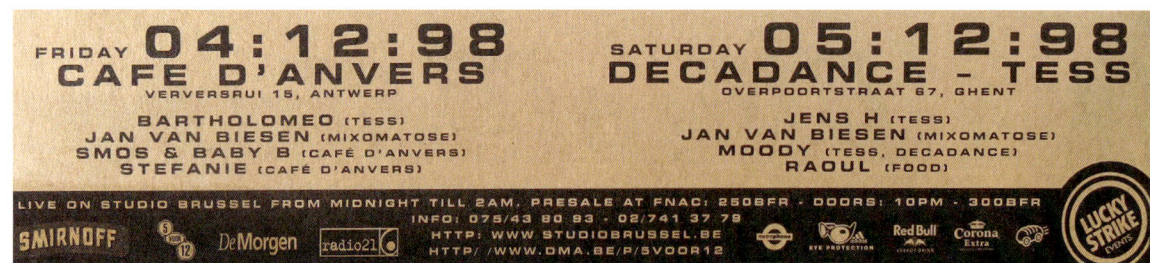

December 1998, *Mixomatose* at Café d'Anvers and Decadance, Antwerp, Ghent, 300 × 70 mm.

Saturday 07. 11. 1998, *Eskimo* at Eskimo Factory, Ghent, 195 × 150 mm.

Saturday 21. 03. 1998, *Super 45 Tours* at Catacombes, Roeselare, 174 × 174 mm.

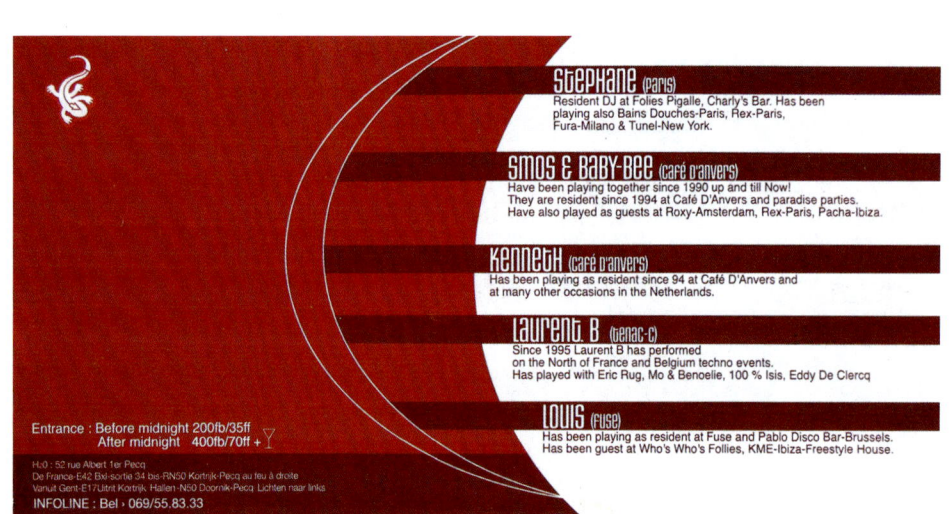

Thursday 30. 04. 1998, H₂0, Pecq, 200 × 100 mm.

Sunday 12. 04. 1998, *Year Of The Tiger*
at Café d'Anvers, Antwerp, 150 × 105 mm.

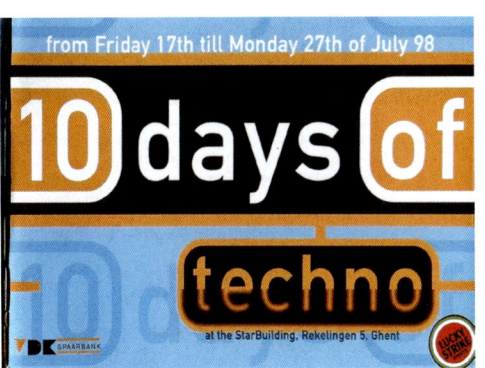

July 1998, *10 days of techno*, Ghent, 150 × 100 mm.

Saturday 05. 12. 1998, *Doctor Strangeluck*
at Atomium, Brussels, 285 × 210 mm.

Friday 25. 09. 1998, Orange,
Scherpenheuvel, 220 × 190 mm.

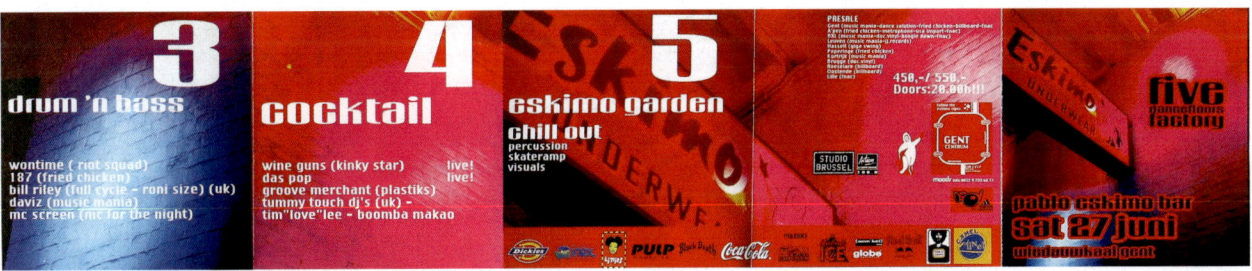

Saturday 27. 06. 1998, *5 Dancefloors Factory* at
Pablo Eskimo Bar, Ghent, 600 × 120 mm.

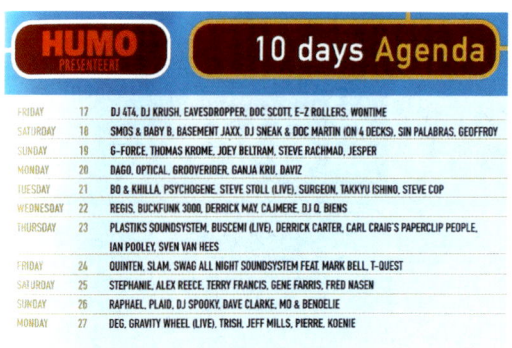

July 1998, *10 days of techno*, Ghent, 150 × 100 mm.

Sunday 12. 04. 1998, *Year Of The Tiger* at Café d'Anvers, Antwerp, 150 × 105 mm.

Friday 25. 09. 1998, Orange, Scherpenheuvel, 220 × 190 mm.

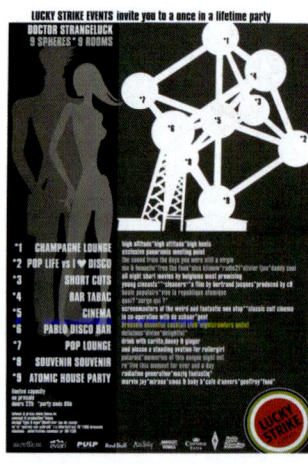

Saturday 05. 12. 1998, *Doctor Strangeluck* at Atomium, Brussels, 285 × 210 mm.

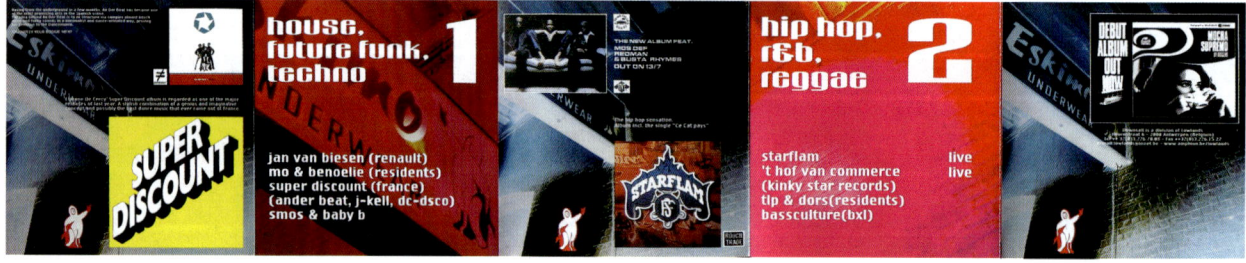

Saturday 27. 06. 1998, *5 Dancefloors Factory* at Pablo Eskimo Bar, Ghent, 600 × 120 mm.

March 1999, Rêve d'O,
Tournai, 295 × 150 mm.

Sunday 04. 04. 1999, *Never Say Never* at Café
d'Anvers, Antwerp, 160 × 105 mm.

Saturday 03. 04. 1999, *Rodeo Eskimo*
at Eskimo Factory, Ghent, 420 × 295 mm.

Saturday 06. 02. 1999, *Wally's Groove World* ↑
at Vino Harto, Antwerp, 85 × 55 mm.

Friday 08. 10. 1999, *Funky City* ↑
at SONIK, Brussels, 280 × 100 mm.

1999

Friday 09. 04. 1999, *Shit Goddamn!*
at Fill Collins Club, Antwerp, 160 × 105 mm.

Saturday 03. 04. 1999, *Rodeo Eskimo*
at Eskimo Factory, Ghent, 420 × 295 mm.

Friday 08. 10. 1999, *Funky City* ↑
at SONIK, Brussels, 280 × 100 mm.

↑ Saturday 06. 02. 1999, *Wally's Groove World*
at Vino Harto, Antwerp, 85 × 55 mm.

March 1999, Rêve d'O, Tournai, 295 × 150 mm.

Saturday 22. 05. 1999, *Pinguin?*, Ghent, 50 × 50 mm.

Wednesday 12. 05. 1999, Rêve d'O, Tournai, 200 × 90 mm.

Saturday 02. 10. 1999, Silo, Leuven, 195 × 145 mm.

Friday 13. 08. 1999, *Post Gent* at Postgebouw Korenmarkt, Ghent, 600 × 200 mm.

1999

SUPERSTAR DJ'S LEVEL ONE HOUSE FUTURE FUNK
TRIXIE SMAK
MO&BENOELIE ESKIMO
GEORGE THOMSON PLASTIC AVENGERS SCOTLAND
DIXON JAZZANOVA RECORDS BERLIN
SMOS&BABY B ESKIMO
SUPERSTAR DJ'S LEVEL TWO COCKTAIL POP LOUNGE
ANDRE PINGUIN PRESIDENT
FLYING DEWAELE BROTHERS SOULWAX
TUTTU MATTO TUMMY TOUCH UK
MR SCRUFF NINJA TUNE UK
LORIN MR. AFRO BEAT
SUPERSTAR DJ'S LEVEL THREE DRUM AND BASS
JUICE BLENDERS MUSIC MANIA
KONFLICT RENEGADE HARDWARE UK
MILLENNIUM KRU ESKIMO
LEVEL FOUR SUPERSTARS' SUPERSTAR VIP LOUNGE
SOUNDSCAPES AND LANDSCAPES COMPILED BY
ANDRE&MO&BENOELIE

HEY BOY, HEY GIRL

saturday 22 may
22h00
wiedauwkaai gent
smos & baby b
& andré
the poodle himself
200,.

doggy style!

Saturday 22. 05. 1999, *Pinguin?*, Ghent, 50 × 50 mm.

March 1999, *Rêve d'O*,
Tournai, 295 × 150 mm.

WEDNESDAY 12 MAY 99

BRANDY
BIRTHDAY MARCO

GUEST
RAOUL [FOOD RÊVE D'O]
SMOS&BABY B [CAFÉ D'ANVERS ESKIMO]
T-QUEST [MUSIC MAN]
GEOFFROY [FOOD-SSR]
KALKY [CATACOMBES RÊVE D'O]
MURVIN JAY [MIRANO FREAKY JAM]

50FF/300FB

CHAUSSÉE DE BRUXELLES - BARRY (TOURNAI)
INFOLINE 00 32 (0)69 548 578 - reved@hotmail.com
OPEN EVERY FRIDAY AT 22H - FREE ENTRANCE
OPEN EVERY SATURDAY AT 22H - 50FF/

FROM LILLE : E42, TOURNAI - EXIT 32, LEUZE - LEUZE N7
FROM BRUXELLES : A8 - ATH - LEUZE - BARRY
FROM ANTWERPEN, GENT, MOUSCRON : E17 - TOURNAI EXIT 32 - LEUZE N7
FOLLOW SKY TRACER !

Wednesday 12. 05. 1999, *Rêve d'O*,
Tournai, 200 × 90 mm.

Friday 25. 06. 1999, *Eskimo* at Eskimo Factory,
Ghent, 420 × 295 mm.

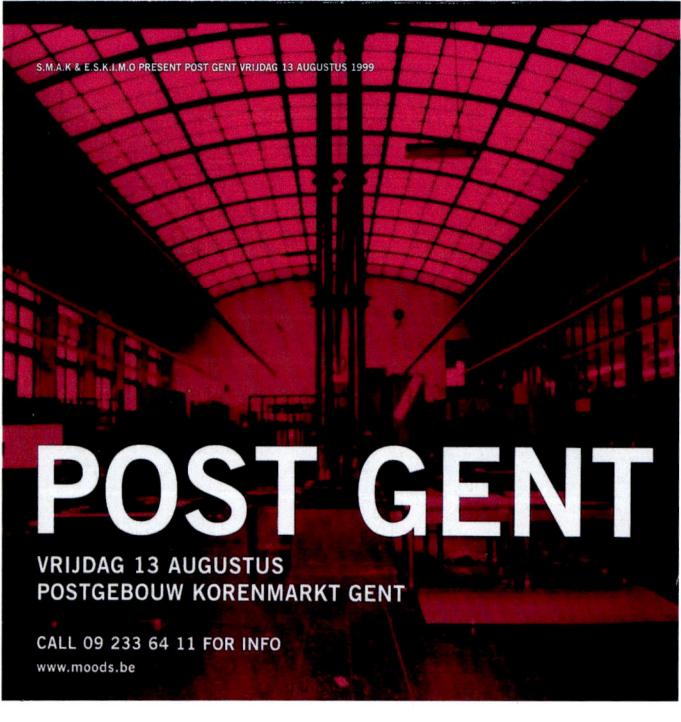

Friday 13. 08. 1999, *Post Gent* at Postgebouw
Korenmarkt, Ghent, 600 × 200 mm.

1999

Saturday 25. 09. 1999, Rêve d'O,
Tournai, 120 × 120 mm.

Sunday 04. 04. 1999, *Detroit Connection*
at VIP Hall Kuipke, Ghent, 210 × 100 mm.

Friday 25. 06. 1999, *Eskimo* at Eskimo Factory,
Ghent, 420 × 295 mm.

Saturday 26. 06. 1999, *Cruises to Pleasure*,
Antwerp, 210 × 147,5 mm.

Saturday 30. 10. 1999, *Fuzz Club* at Ciné Café,
Herentals, 150 × 150 mm.

Friday 30. 04. 1999, *One year of
Ondulation* at Sonik, Brussels, 200 × 150 mm.

Sunday 04. 04. 1999, *Detroit Connection* at VIP Hall Kuipke, Ghent, 210 × 100 mm.

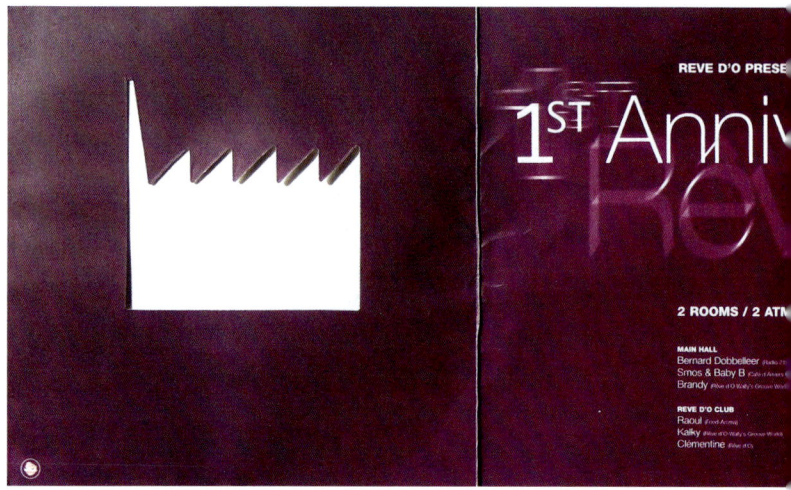

Saturday 25. 09. 1999, Rêve d'O, Tournai, 120 × 120 mm.

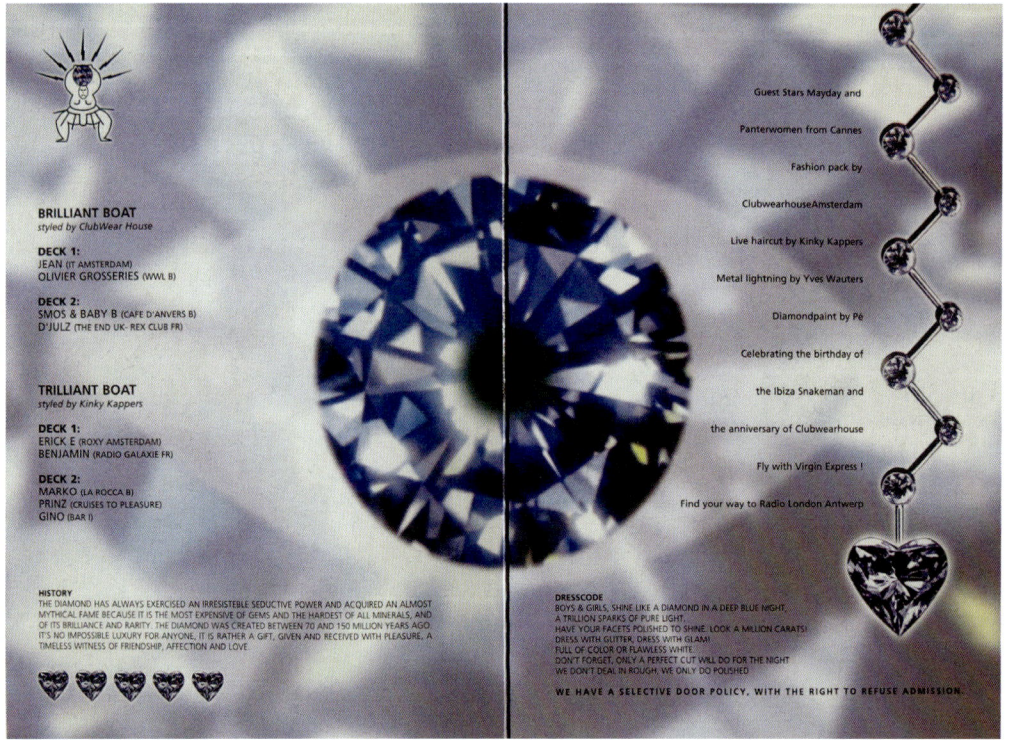

Saturday 26. 06. 1999, *Cruises to Pleasure*, Antwerp, 210 × 147,5 mm.

Friday 30. 04. 1999, *One year of Ondulation* at Sonik, Brussels, 200 × 150 mm.

Saturday 30. 10. 1999, *Fuzz Club* at Ciné Café, Herentals, 150 × 150 mm.

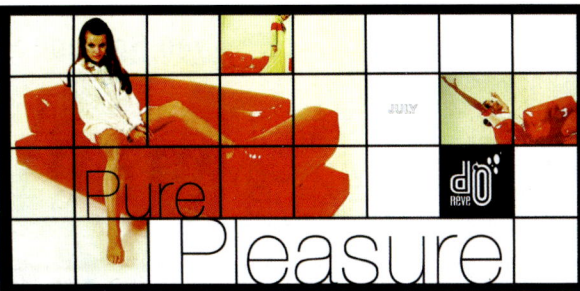

July 1999, Rêve d'O, Tournai, 210 × 100 mm.

WHY DON'T YOU BRING YOUR SISTER AND YOUR MOTHER AND YOUR FATHER TOO ? POST2000

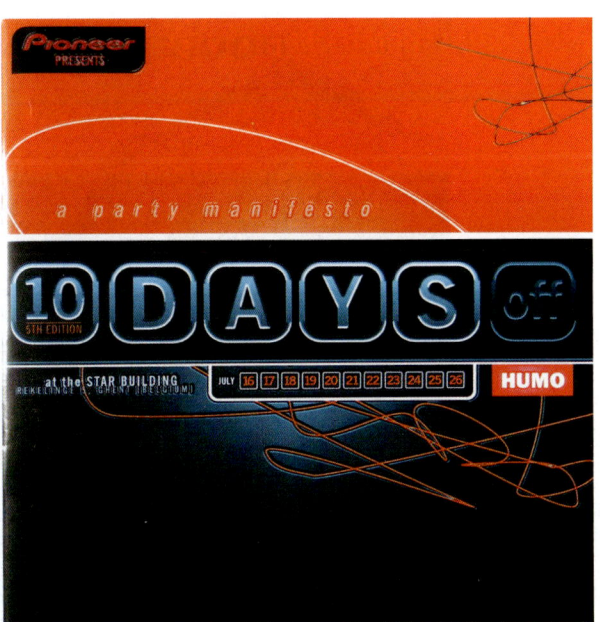

Friday 31. 12. 1999, *POST 2000*, Ghent, 410 × 140 mm.

July 1999, *10 days off*, Ghent, 200 × 200 mm.

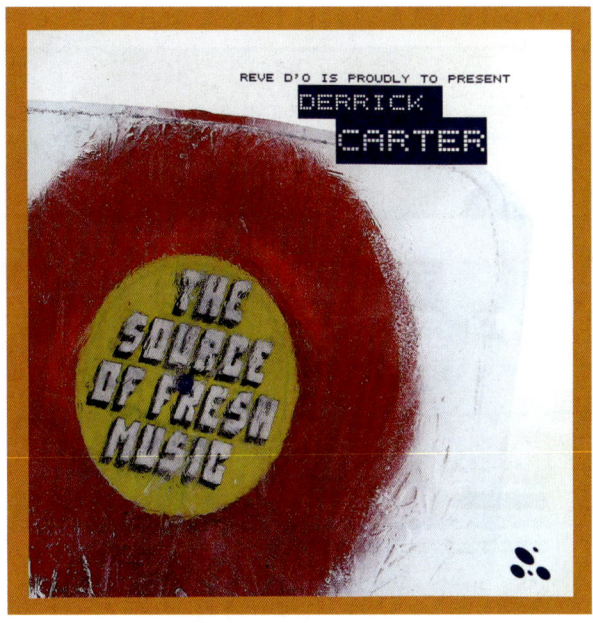

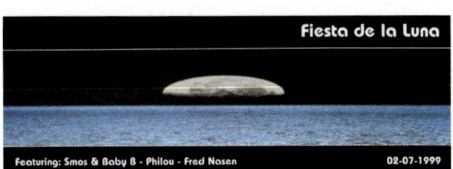

Friday 02. 07. 1999, *Fiesta de la Luna* at Zeilclub RBSC, Heusden, 210 × 73 mm.

Saturday 22. 05. 1999, Rêve d'O, Tournai, 200 × 200 mm.

POST 2000
FRIDAY 31 DECEMBER
KORENMARKT GENT
FROM 23.00 TILL 09.00
ANDRE
MO&BENOELIE
SMOS&BABY B
TLP&DORS
FLYING DEWAELE BROS

ESKIMO EXCLUSIVE
POST 2000
SOUNDTRACK BY
MO
BENOELIE
ANDRE
SMOS
BABY B
FLYING
DEWAELE
BROTHERS
TLP
DORS

FRIDAY 31 DECEMBER
KORENMARKT GENT

POSTCARD 2000 USE ME

Friday 31. 12. 1999, *POST 2000*, Ghent, 410 × 140 mm.

Saturday 22. 05. 1999, Rêve d'O, Tournai, 200 × 200 mm.

Saturday 06. 03. 1999, *Eskimo* at Eskimo Factory, Ghent, 600 × 120 mm.

July 1999, Rêve d'O, Tournai, 210 × 100 mm.

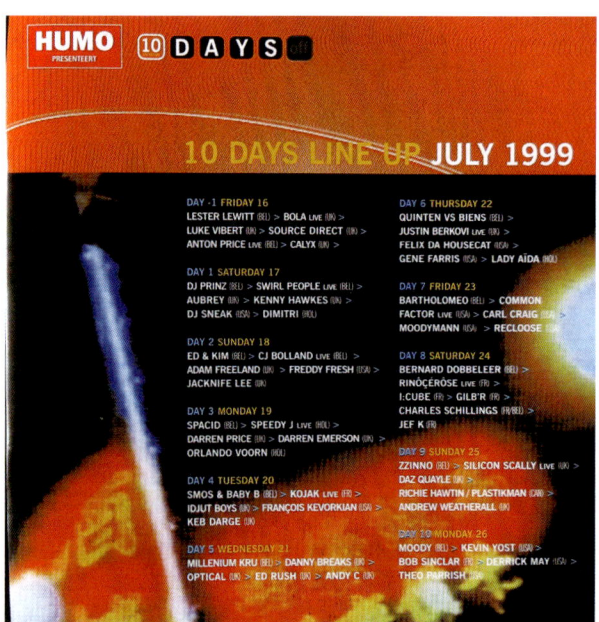

July 1999, *10 days off*, Ghent, 200 × 200 mm.

Friday 02. 07. 1999, *Fiesta de la Luna* at Zeilclub RBSC, Heusden, 210 × 73 mm.

May 1999, Launch, Machelen - Deinze, 375 × 105 mm.

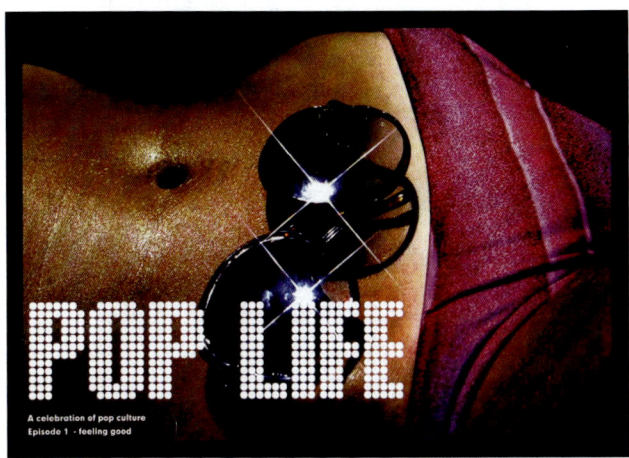

Saturday 30. 01. 1999, *Pop Life* at Studio 99, Ghent, 300 × 210 mm.

Wednesday 10. 11. 1999, *Eskimo* at Eskimo Factory, Ghent, 600 × 420 mm.

March 1999, Decadance, → Ghent, 240 × 160 mm.

Saturday 16. 10. 1999, → *Cruises to Pleasure*, Antwerp, 295 × 210 mm.

Friday 19. 11. 1999, *100% vinyl* at Rumba & Co, Leuven, 140 × 100 mm.

1999

Wednesday 10. 11. 1999, *Eskimo* at Eskimo Factory, Ghent, 600 × 420 mm.

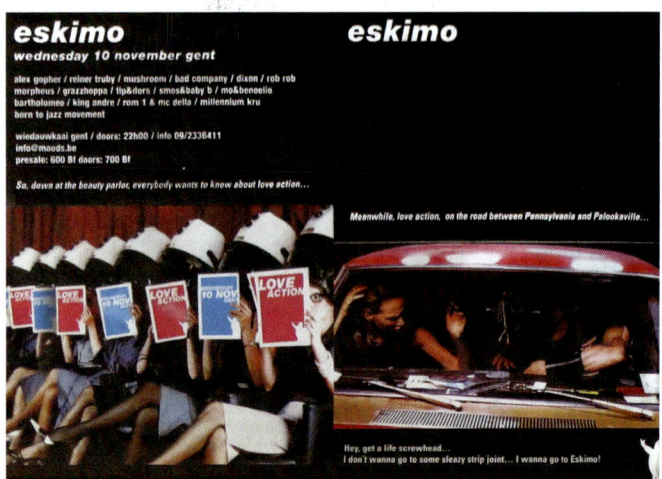

May 1999, Launch, Machelen - Deinze, 375 × 105 mm.

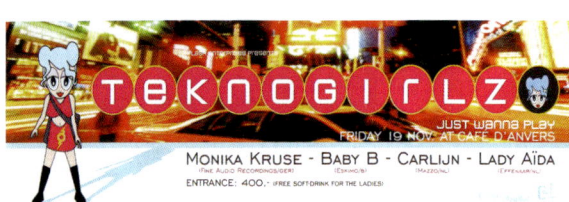

Friday 19. 11. 1999, *Teknogirlz* at Café d'Anvers, Antwerp, 185 × 550 mm.

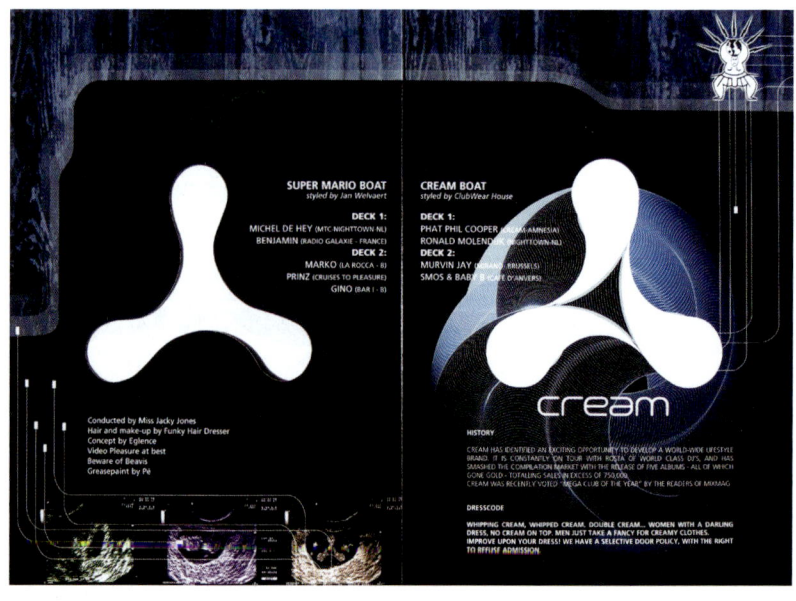

Saturday 30. 01. 1999, *Pop Life* at Studio 99, Ghent, 300 × 210 mm.

↑ March 1999, Decadance, Ghent, 240 × 160 mm.

Saturday 16. 10. 1999, → *Cruises to Pleasure*, Antwerp, 295 × 210 mm.

Saturday 06. 03. 1999, *Eskimo*
at Eskimo Factory, Ghent, 600 × 120 mm.

Saturday 24. 06. 2000, *Eskimo*
at Eskimo Factory, Ghent, 340 × 170 mm.

Saturday 26. 02. 2000, *Oase De Pleasure* at Den Hemel, Zichem, 210 × 150 mm.

Saturday 01. 01. 2000, *Cruises To Pleasure*, Antwerp, 210 × 150 mm.

April 2000, *Saturdays* at Café d'Anvers, Antwerp, 103 × 103 mm.

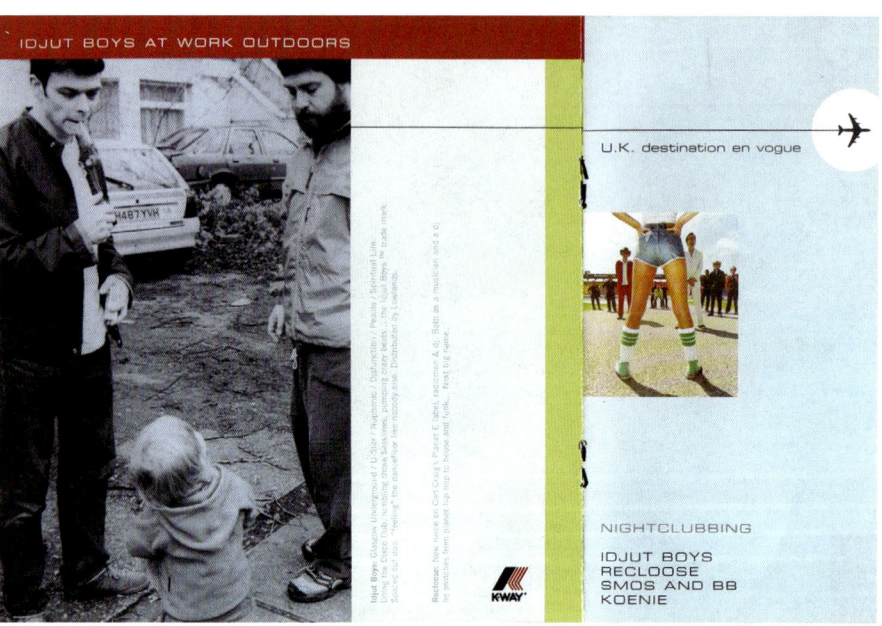

Saturday 24. 06. 2000, *Eskimo* at Eskimo Factory, Ghent, 340 × 170 mm.

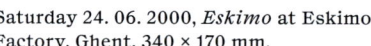

Saturday 01. 01. 2000, *Cruises To Pleasure*, Antwerp, 210 × 150 mm.

April 2000, *Saturdays* at Café d'Anvers, Antwerp, 103 × 103 mm.

Sunday 02. 07. 2000, Diesel at Café d'Anvers, Antwerp, 480 × 175 mm.

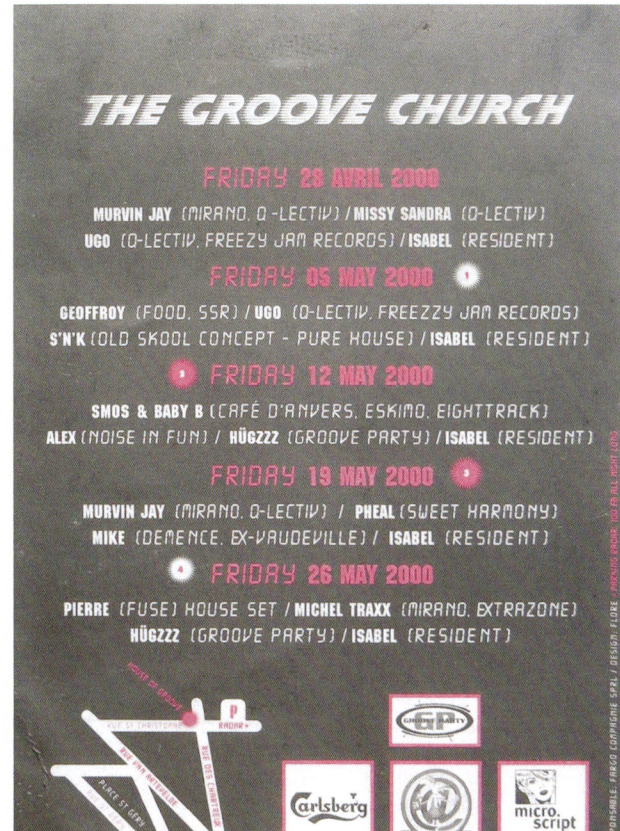

Friday 12. 05. 2000, *The House Of Groove* at The Groove Church, Brussels, 150 × 105 mm.

Saturday 25. 03. 2000, *On*, Brussels, 210 × 150 mm.

Saturday 29. 01. 2000, *Night Of The Loud Records* at Gildenhuis, Meerhout, 300 × 150 mm.

Friday 31. 03. 2000, *Movida* at Ric's Boat, Brussels, 145 × 47 mm.

Saturday 29. 07. 2000, *Midsummer Dance*, Dendermonde, 300 × 110 mm.

Friday 12. 05. 2000, *The House Of Groove* at The Groove Church, Brussels, 150 × 105 mm.

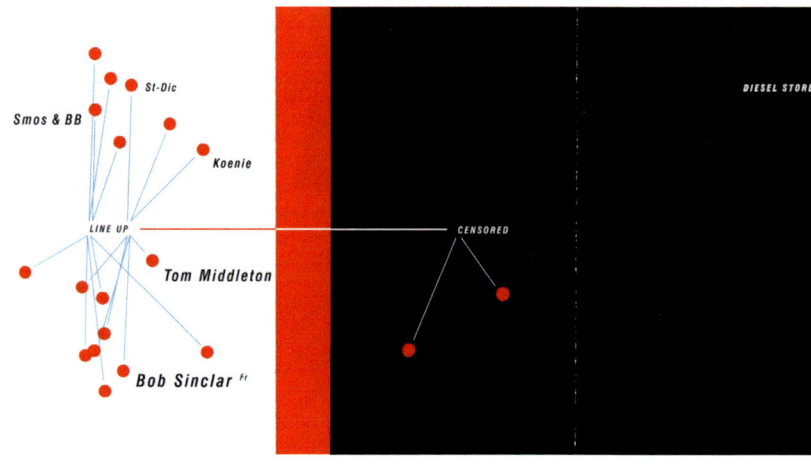

Sunday 02. 07. 2000, *Diesel* at Café d'Anvers, Antwerp, 480 × 175 mm.

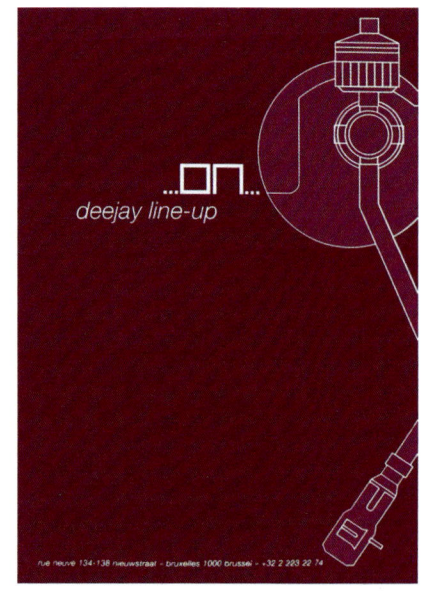

Saturday 25. 03. 2000, *On*, Brussels, 210 × 150 mm.

Friday 31. 03. 2000, *Movida* at Ric's Boat, Brussels, 145 × 47 mm.

Saturday 29. 07. 2000, *Midsummer Dance*, Dendermonde, 300 × 110 mm.

Friday 06. 10. 2000, *Disco 2000*
at Café d'Anvers, Antwerp, 140 × 140 mm.

Saturday 30. 12. 2000, *Cruises To Pleasure*,
Antwerp, 300 × 120 mm.

Friday 28. 04. 2000,
Rhum Road at
St-Gé Club, Brussels,
200 × 60 mm.

Friday 14. 07. 2000, *Natural Sound*
at Zoo, Tournai, 150 × 150 mm.

July 2000, *10 days off*, Ghent, 180 × 180 mm.

October 2000, Café d'Anvers,
Antwerp, 280 × 140 mm.

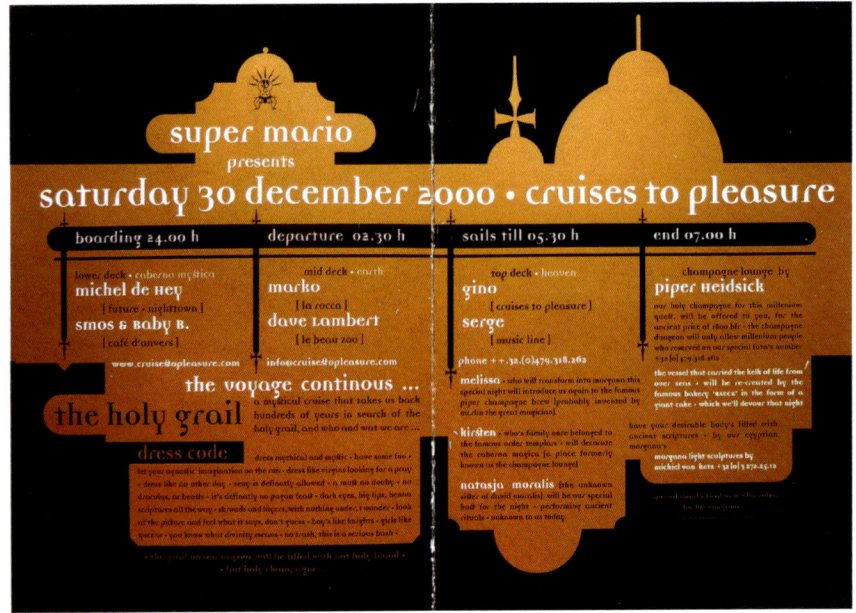

Saturday 30. 12. 2000, *Cruises To Pleasure*, Antwerp, 300 × 120 mm.

Friday 06. 10. 2000, *Disco 2000* at Café d'Anvers, Antwerp, 140 × 140 mm.

Friday 28. 04. 2000, *Rhum Road* at St-Gé Club, Brussels, 200 × 60 mm.

July 2000, *10 days off*, Ghent, 180 × 180 mm.

Friday 14. 07. 2000, *Natural Sound* at Zoo, Tournai, 150 × 150 mm.

October 2000, Café d'Anvers, Antwerp, 280 × 140 mm.

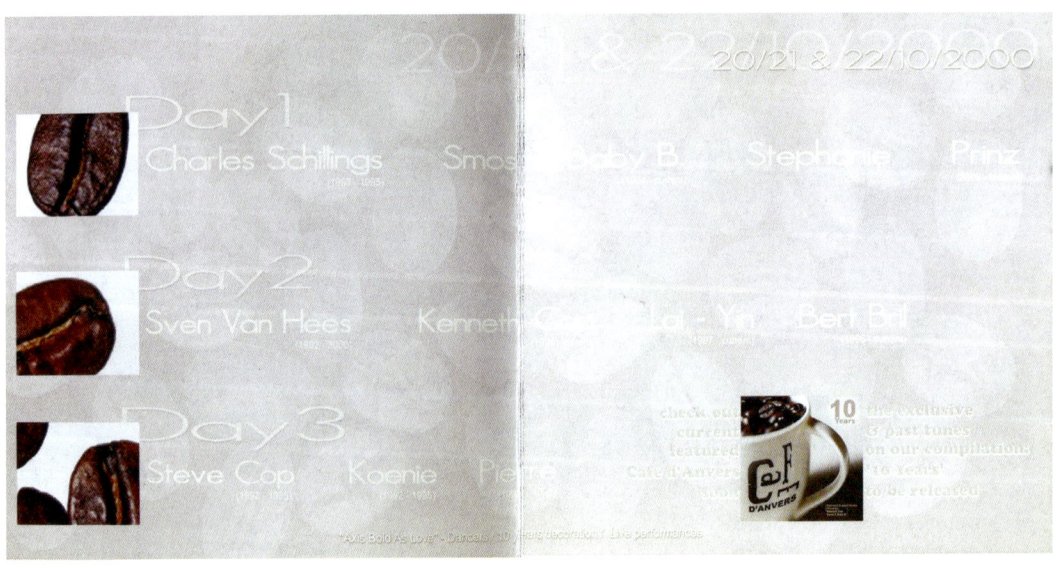

November 2000, Club Geluk, Antwerp, 125 × 125 mm.

Friday 30. 06. 2000, *Never Say Never* at Fill Collins Club and Café d'Anvers, Antwerp, 285 × 190 mm.

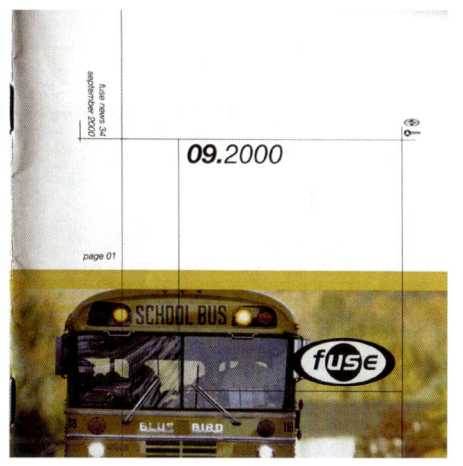

September 2000, Fuse, Brussels, 120 × 120 mm.

Friday 05. 05. 2000, *Movin'* at Cherry Moon, Lokeren, 210 × 95 mm.

July 2000, Fuse, Brussels, 120 × 120 mm.

Sunday 31. 12. 2000, Café d'Anvers, Antwerp, 195 × 195 mm.

November 2000, Club Geluk, Antwerp, 125 × 125 mm.

Friday 30. 06. 2000, *Never Say Never* at Fill Collins Club and Café d'Anvers, Antwerp, 285 × 190 mm.

Friday 05. 05. 2000, *Movin'* at Cherry Moon, Lokeren, 210 × 95 mm.

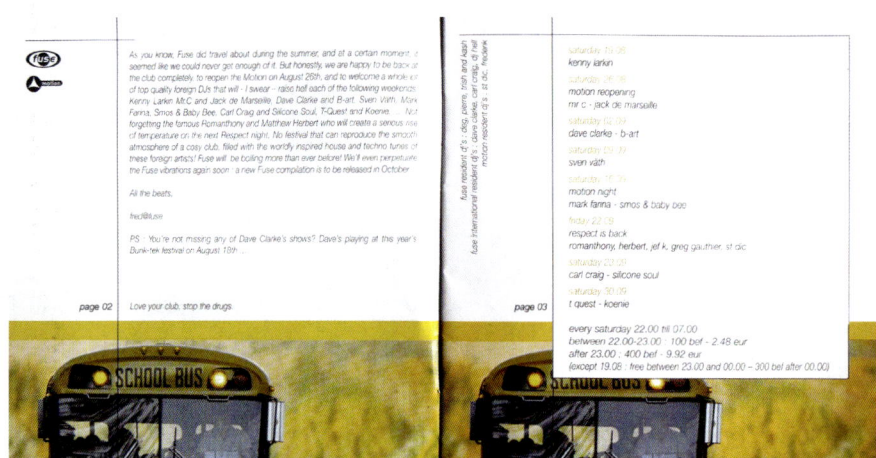

September 2000, Fuse, Brussels, 120 × 120 mm.

Sunday 31. 12. 2000, Café d'Anvers, Antwerp, 195 × 195 mm.

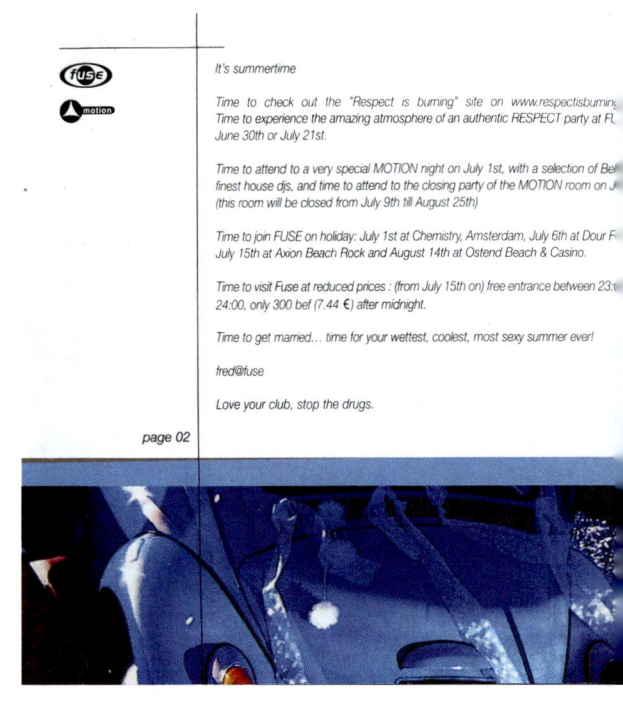

July 2000, Fuse, Brussels, 120 × 120 mm.

84 2000

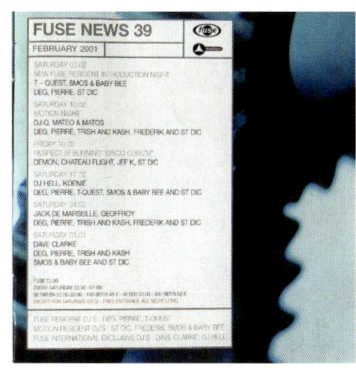

February 2001, Fuse, Brussels, 120 × 120 mm.

Saturday 24. 02. 2001, *Bel Mondo* at SMAK, Ghent, 230 × 170 mm.

Saturday 03. 02. 2001, *New Fuse resident introduction night* at Fuse, Brussels, 120 × 120 mm.

Saturday 27. 01. 2001, *Fuse On Tour*, Brussels, 120 × 120 mm.

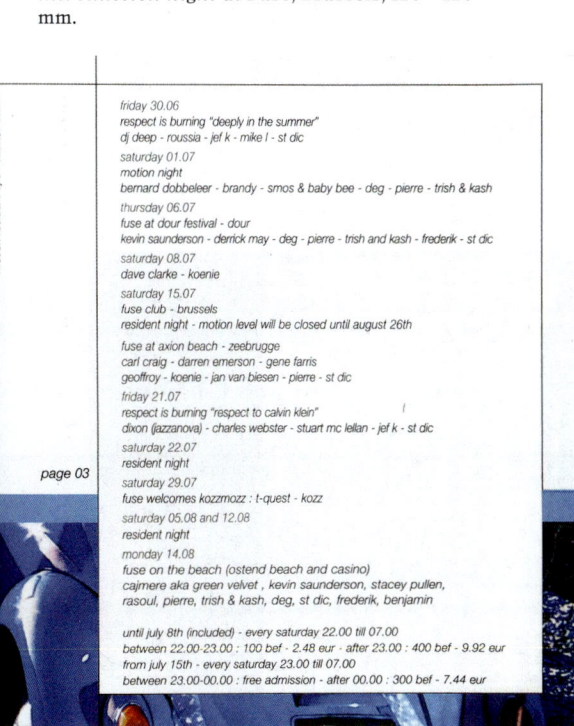

Saturday 27. 01. 2001, *Fuse On Tour*, Brussels, 120 × 120 mm.

2001

Saturday 24. 02. 2001, *Bel Mondo* at SMAK, Ghent, 230 × 170 mm.

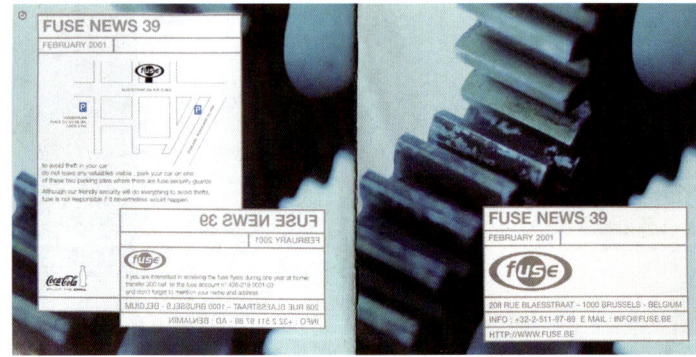

February 2001, Fuse, Brussels, 120 × 120 mm.

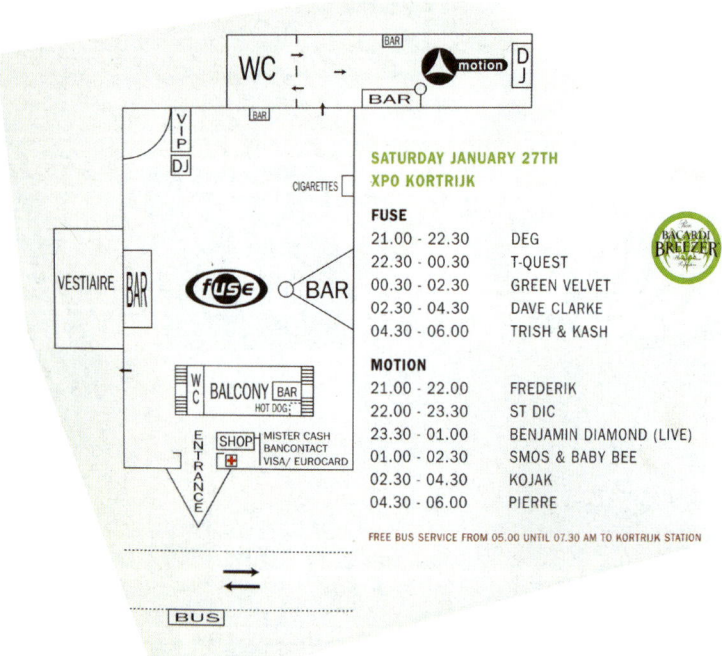

Saturday 27. 01. 2001, *Fuse On Tour*, Brussels, 120 × 120 mm.

Saturday 17. 02. 2001, Fuse, Brussels, 120 × 120 mm.

Saturday 27. 01. 2001, *Fuse On Tour*, Brussels, 120 × 120 mm.

Saturday 27. 01. 2001, *Fuse On Tour*, Brussels, 120 × 120 mm.

March 2001, Fuse, Brussels, 120 × 120 mm.

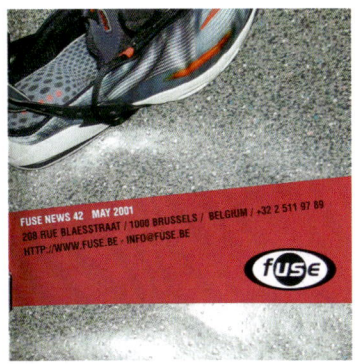

May 2001, Fuse, Brussels, 120 × 120 mm.

April 2001, Fuse, Brussels, 120 × 120 mm.

Saturday 03. 03. 2001, Fuse, Brussels, 120 × 120 mm.

May & June 2001, *Food* at Silo, Leuven, 210 × 150 mm.

Friday 01. 06. 2001, *Buddha Bar* at Café d'Anvers, Antwerp, 150 × 105 mm.

March 2001, Fuse, Brussels, 120 × 120 mm.

April 2001, Fuse, Brussels, 120 × 120 mm.

May 2001, Fuse, Brussels, 120 × 120 mm.

Saturday 26. 05. 2001, Fuse, Brussels, 120 × 120 mm.

Friday 01. 06. 2001, *Buddha Bar* at Café d'Anvers, Antwerp, 150 × 105 mm.

May & June 2001, *Food* at Silo, Leuven, 210 × 150 mm.

Friday 11. 05. 2001, *Moviida* at Who's Who's Land, Brussels, 150 × 150 mm.

Friday 29. 06. 2001, *Midnight Garden* at T-Rex Estate, Schoten, 210 × 150 mm.

June 2001, Fuse, Brussels, 120 × 120 mm.

Sunday 03. 06. 2001, *Stars & Stripes* at Café d'Anvers, Antwerp, 210 × 150 mm.

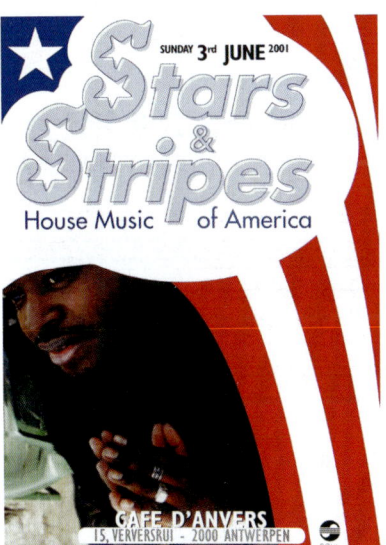

June 2001, Fuse, Brussels, 120 × 120 mm.

30. 06.– 01. 07. 2001, *House Torhout*, Torhout, 295 × 210 mm.

Friday 29. 06. 2001, *Midnight Garden* at T-Rex Estate, Schoten, 210 × 150 mm.

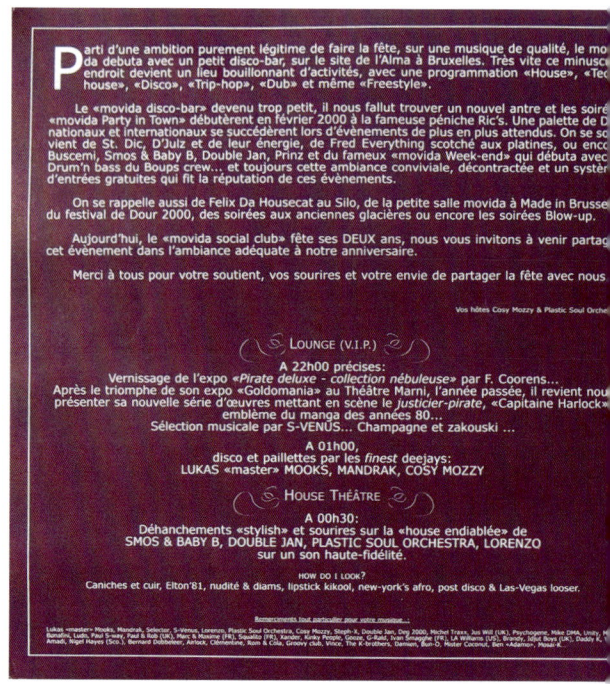

Friday 11. 05. 2001, *Moviida* at Who's Who's Land, Brussels, 150 × 150 mm.

June 2001, Fuse, Brussels, 120 × 120 mm.

30. 06.– 01. 07. 2001, *House Torhout*, Torhout, 295 × 210 mm.

Sunday 03. 06. 2001, *Stars & Stripes* at Café d'Anvers, Antwerp, 210 × 150 mm.

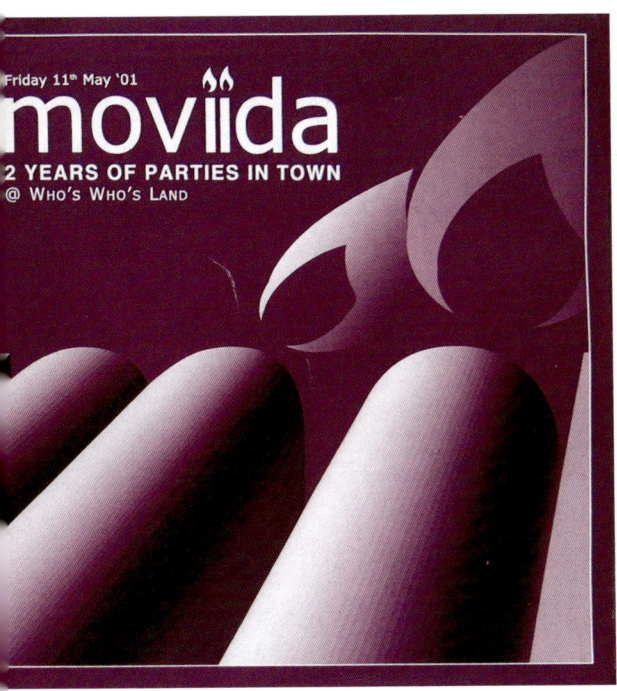

14.–23. 07. 2001, 10 days off, Ghent, 300 × 300 mm.

31. 08.–01. 09. 2001, Liverpool
Aan De Schelde, Antwerp, 133 × 93 mm.

Summer 2001, Fuse, Brussels, 120 × 120 mm.

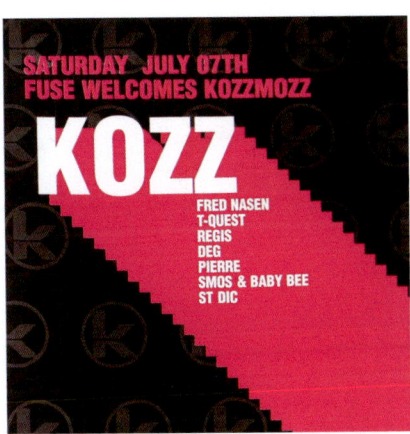

Saturday 07. 07. 2001, *Fuse welcomes Kozzmozz* at Fuse, Brussels, 120 × 120 mm.

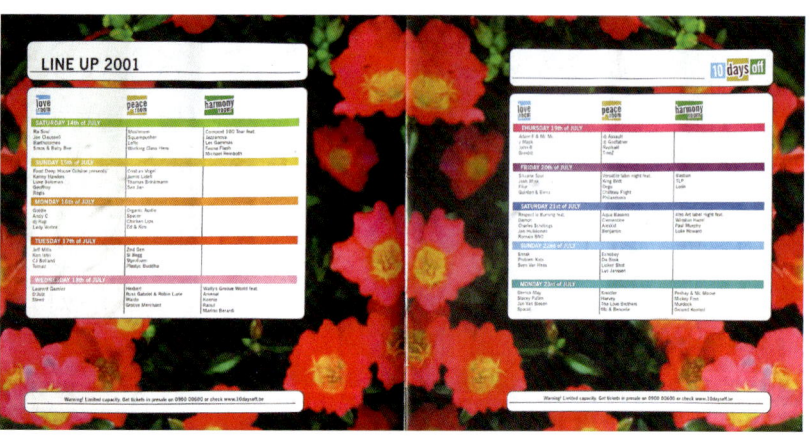

14.–23. 07. 2001, 10 days off, Ghent, 300 × 300 mm.

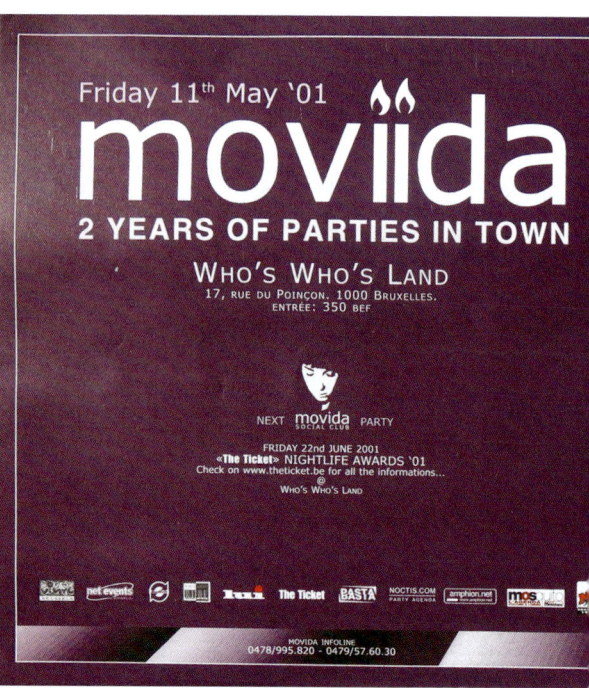

Friday 11. 05. 2001, *Moviida* at
Who's Who's Land, Brussels, 150 × 150 mm.

Saturday 23. 06. 2001, Fuse,
Brussels, 120 × 120 mm.

31. 08.–01. 09. 2001, Liverpool
Aan De Schelde, Antwerp, 133 × 93 mm.

Summer 2001, Fuse, Brussels, 120 × 120 mm.

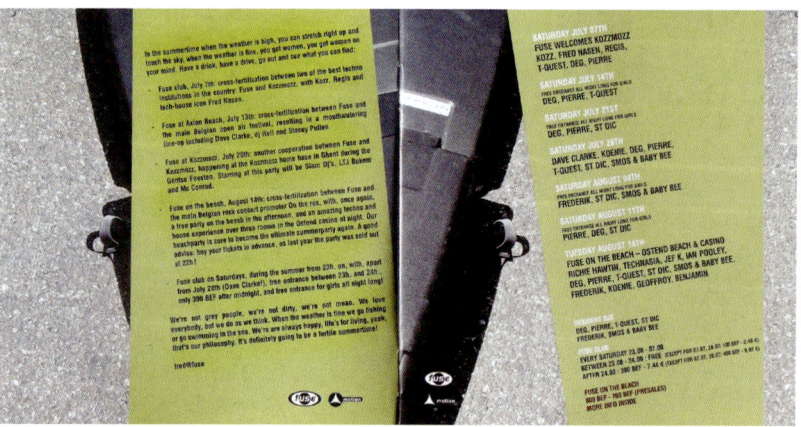

Friday 28. 09. 2001, *Technics*
at Café d'Anvers, Antwerp, 150 × 105 mm.

Saturday 25. 08. 2001, Fuse,
Brussels, 120 × 120 mm.

Tuesday 14. 08. 2001, *Fuse On The Beach*
at Ostend Beach & Casino, Ostend, 210 × 150 mm.

Friday 10. 08. 2001, Clubland,
Antwerp, 420 × 150 mm.

September 2001, Fuse,
Brussels, 120 × 120 mm.

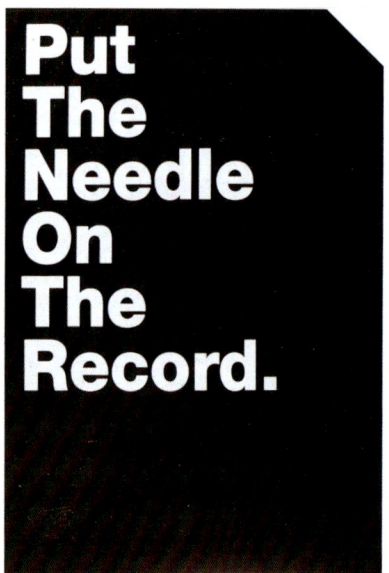

Friday 28. 09. 2001, *Technics*
at Café d'Anvers, Antwerp, 150 × 105 mm.

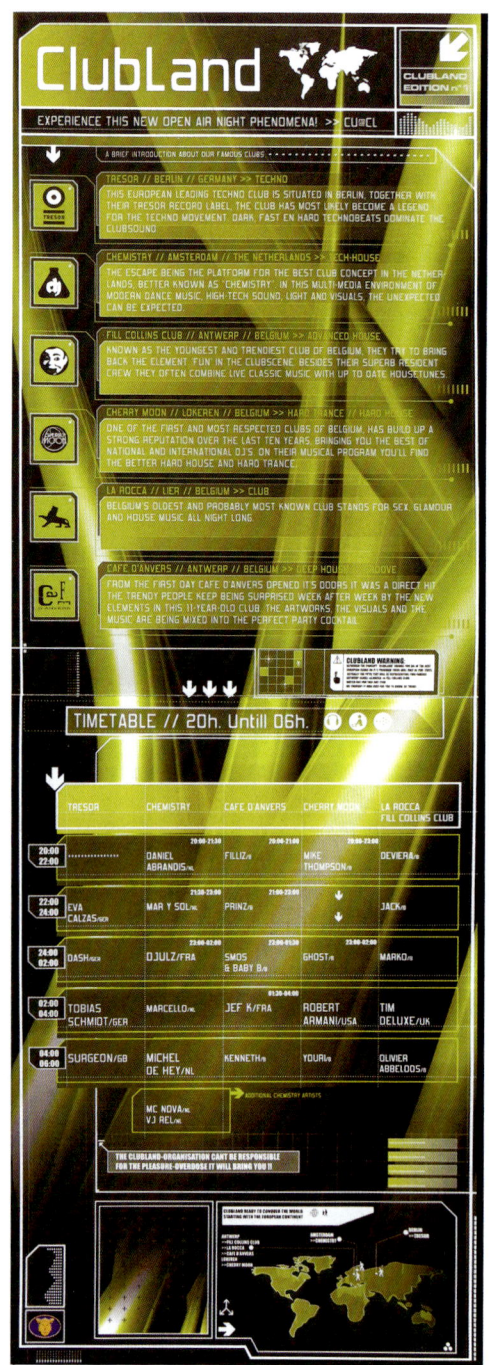

Friday 10. 08. 2001, Clubland,
Antwerp, 420 × 150 mm.

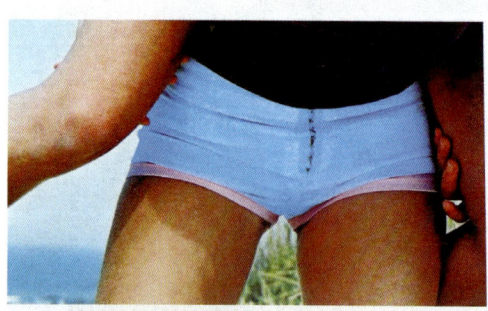

Tuesday 14. 08. 2001, *Fuse On The Beach*
at Ostend Beach & Casino, Ostend, 210 × 150 mm.

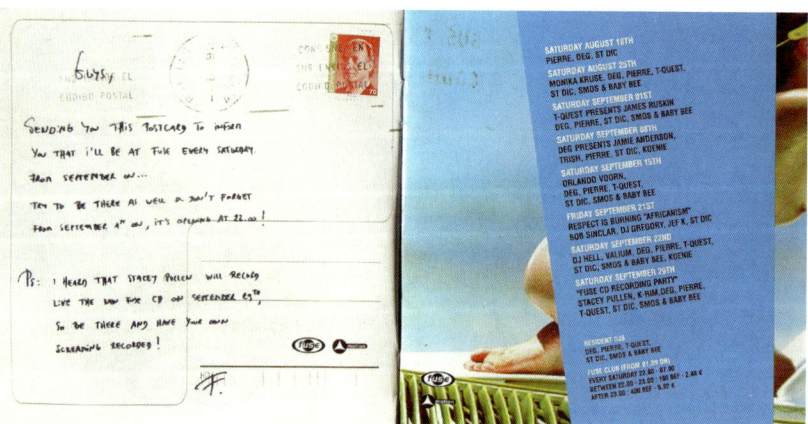

September 2001, Fuse,
Brussels, 120 × 120 mm.

2001

Tuesday 16. 10. 2001, *Stars & Stripes* at Café d'Anvers, Antwerp, 150 × 105 mm.

Saturday 08. 09. 2001, *Laundry Day*, Antwerp, 150 × 105 mm.

Saturday 29. 09. 2001, Fuse, Brussels, 120 × 120 mm.

October, November & December 2001, Fuse, Brussels, 285 × 140 mm.

Friday 12. 10. 2001, *E-motion*
at Silo, Leuven, 200 × 72 mm.

September, October & November 2001,
Fuse, Brussels, 285 × 140 mm.

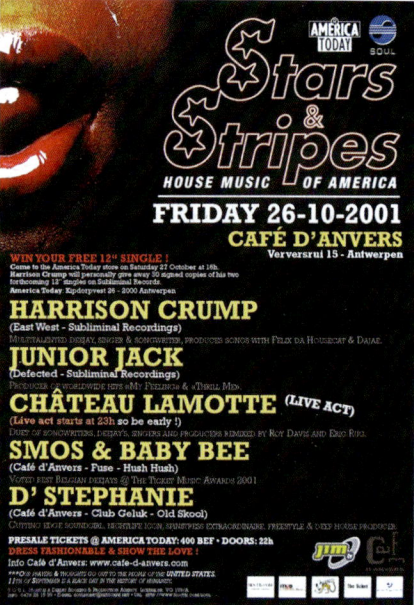

Tuesday 16. 10. 2001, *Stars & Stripes*
at Café d'Anvers, Antwerp, 150 × 105 mm.

Saturday 01. 09. 2001, Fuse,
Brussels, 120 × 120 mm.

Friday 07. 12. 2001, *The Untouchables* at Café d'Anvers, Antwerp, 150 × 105 mm.

Sunday 31. 12. 2001, Fuse, Brussels, 120 × 120 mm.

December 2001, Café d'Anvers, Antwerp, 140 × 140 mm.

December 2001, Fuse, Brussels, 375 × 140 mm.

October & November 2001, *Fataal* at Musicafé, Leuven, 150 × 100 mm.

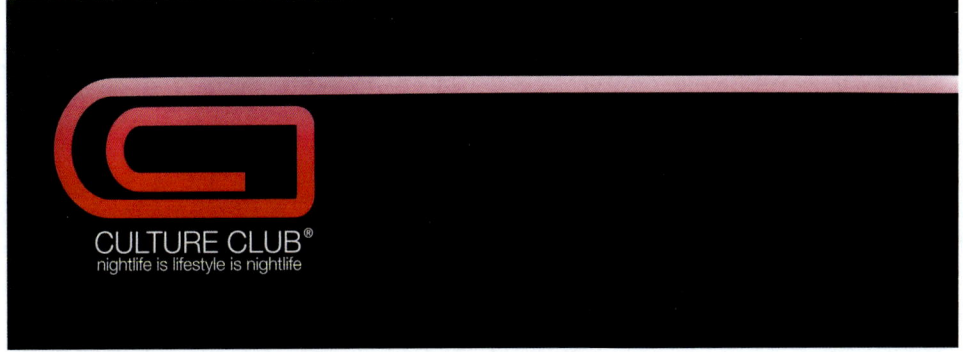

November 2001, Culture Club, Ghent, 340 × 120 mm.

December 2001, Fuse, Brussels, 375 × 140 mm.

Friday 07. 12. 2001, *The Untouchables* at Café d'Anvers, Antwerp, 150 × 105 mm.

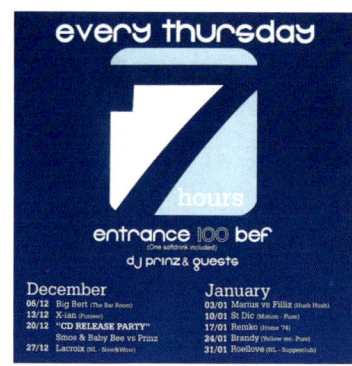

December 2001, Café d'Anvers, Antwerp, 140 × 140 mm.

October & November 2001, *Fataal* at Musicafé, Leuven, 150 × 100 mm.

November 2001, Culture Club, Ghent, 340 × 120 mm.

February 2002, Fuse,
Brussels, 140 × 95 mm.

January 2002, Fuse,
Brussels, 140 × 95 mm.

Saturday 26. 01. 2002, *Fuse On Tour*
at XPO, Kortrijk, 210 × 150 mm.

Saturday 02.02.
Smos & Baby Bee present
D'Julz
Tomaz

Now and again our residents invite a DJ, that according to them has a certain talent. This time Smos & Baby Bee have invited D'Julz. D'Julz is one of the best known French DJs and one of the very few who started to follow house/techno music in France from it's very beginning. His sets demonstrate the mixing skills and eclectic choice which are the hallmark of the big DJs who play an open-minded selection of good dancing music at parties all over the world. His new compilation is out now on French label "Magic garden". His DJ set will definitely not disappoint even the most difficult to please as he always finds the way to move the dance floor with his unique style.

: T-Quest, Deg : Smos & Baby Bee, St. Dic (Pierre will be playing in Johannesburg, South Africa)
22h till 23h : 2.50 € - after 23h : 10.00 €

Saturday 09.02.
Michel De Heij
Secret Cinema live
Scott Bradford (Lexicon ave. - Shindig)
Frederik

Since '95 Michel De Heij has his own club night in Rotterdam, he's the owner of three record labels such as EC and Brave New World and he got voted plenty of times best dj of The Netherlands. Check www.micheldeheij.nl for everything about this Dutch master of funky techno and enjoy the wicked animations!

You don't have Secret Cinema's debut album 'White Men Can't Funk' in your collection yet? We're pretty sure that you won't have to admit that anymore after you've seen his terrific live set at Fuse. Of course he can funk! By the way, Jeroen Verheij is also the man behind Grooveyard, together with Michel De Heij producer of the absolute classic 'Compound'.

Scott has always been pretty busy in the studio. Setting up the now defunct shiding label (which discovered the happy clappers - I believe). He is heavily involved with owning and running forensic records, putting out quality deep and jazzy house music. This label is rapidly gaining worldwide respect with large export figures and a lot of positive feedback from some well-respected overseas dj's. Scott also records as New Phunk Theory, Little Green Men and Third Movement (with Chris Scott) and as Lexicon Avenue (with Chris and Mark Armstrong) for labels such as Paper Recordings, Yoshitoshi, Airtight and of course Forensic. It is due to these recording projects that Scott can be found guest djing all over the world.

: Pierre, Deg, T-Quest : St. Dic
22h till 23h : 2.50 € - after 23h : 10.00 €

Saturday 16.02.
Motion Night
Kenny Hawkes
Brett Johnson

Brett Johnson has played all over the United States with many of world's top Djs and producers, where he's well known on the West Coast circuit, and has played with the likes of Joshua (Iz), Solar, Jonene from Panhandle, Derrick Carter, Mark Grant, and Mark Farina to name but a few… Over the last 3 years he's been co-running Aesoteric records with his friend Mark Garey. Along with his own music they have released excellent tracks from such artists as JT Donaldson (2nd shift), Tim Shumaker (2nd shift, Home & Garden), Iz & Diz, Cpen , Hakan Lidbo , and Lance Desardi. His music finds favours from the likes of Derrick Carter & Luke Solomon, Kenny Hawkes, Harri & Domenic Cappello from the Sub Club in Glasgow, Jef K and David Duriez from Paris to name but a few…. He's currently recording on Classic (Derrick Carter and Luke Solomon's label), Seasons, Icon, Panhandle, and just recently Hi-phen Music Delivery, a new label from Brussels.

: St.Dic, Smos and Baby Bee
: Pierre, Deg, T-Quest
22h till 23h : 2.50 € - after 23h : 10.00 €

Saturday 23.02.
Revelation Night

Keep on expecting the unexpected

22h-23h : free entrance - after 23h : 7.00 €

Saturday 02.03.
Charles Siegling
Luke Solomon

Fuse is very proud to be able to present to you tonight the first in a row of four of our international residents for 2002: Charles Siegling! Together with Amil Khan he is the driving force behind Technasia, author of the world widely highly acclaimed album 'Future Mix' (voted best album of 2001 by Out Soon). Charles recently released a mix compilation titled 'Plus', a must have in your collection because of the exquisite tracks on it and Charles' wicked mixing skills… to be witnessed live in Fuse!

: Pierre, Deg, T-Quest
: St. Dic, Smos and Baby Bee
22h till 23h : 2.50 € - after 23h : 10.00 €

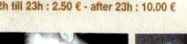

February 2002, Fuse,
Brussels, 140 × 95 mm.

Saturday 26.01.2002, Fuse On Tour
at XPO, Kortrijk, 210 × 150 mm.

January 2002, Fuse,
Brussels, 140 × 95 mm.

Saturday 16. 02. 2002,
Pure, Tournai, 295 × 205 mm.

March 2002, Fuse,
Brussels, 140 × 95 mm.

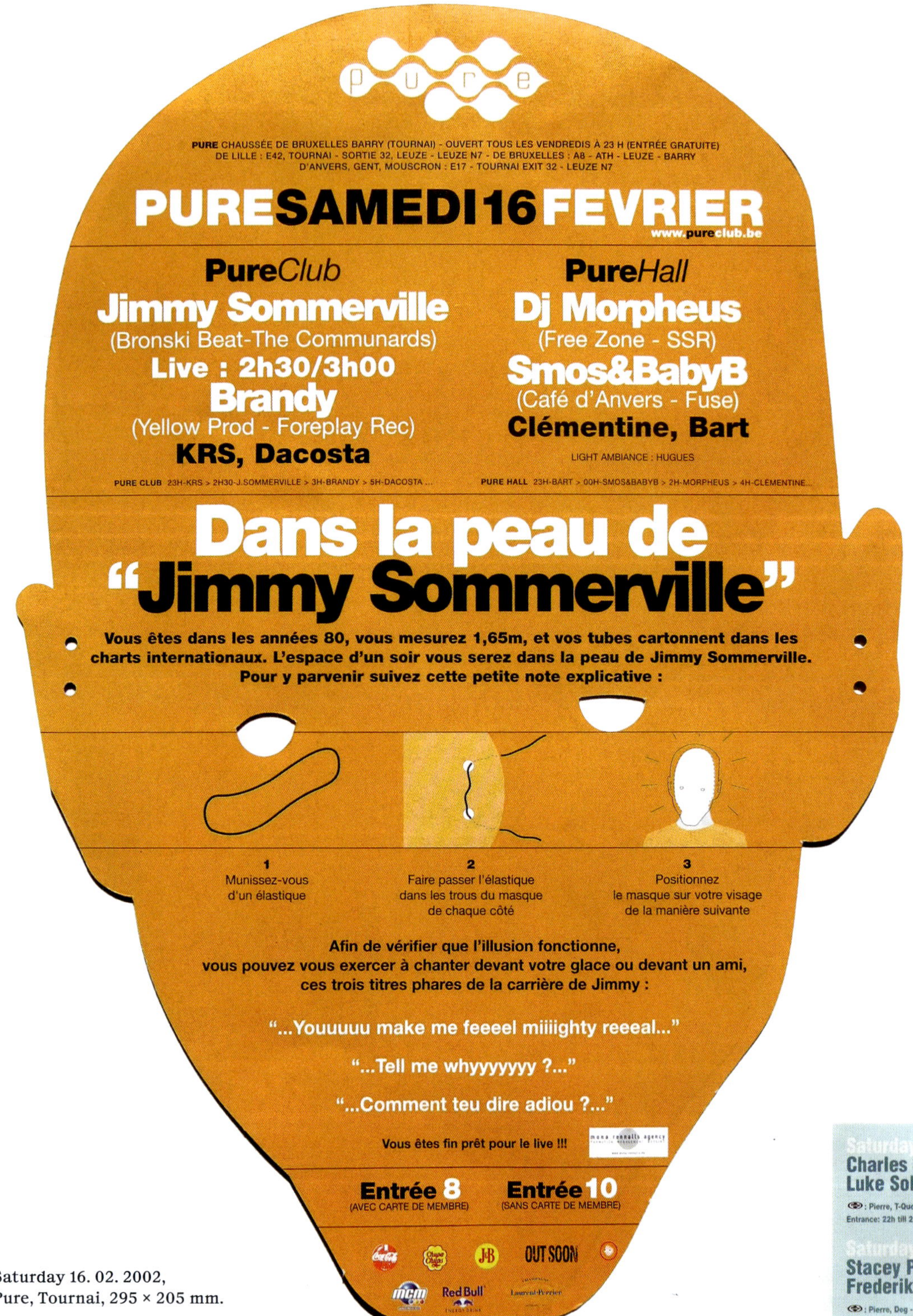
pure
PURE CHAUSSÉE DE BRUXELLES BARRY (TOURNAI) - OUVERT TOUS LES VENDREDIS À 23 H (ENTRÉE GRATUITE)
DE LILLE : E42, TOURNAI - SORTIE 32, LEUZE - LEUZE N7 - DE BRUXELLES : A8 - ATH - LEUZE - BARRY
D'ANVERS, GENT, MOUSCRON : E17 - TOURNAI EXIT 32 - LEUZE N7
PURESAMEDI16FEVRIER
www.pureclub.be
PureClub
Jimmy Sommerville
(Bronski Beat-The Communards)
Live : 2h30/3h00
Brandy
(Yellow Prod - Foreplay Rec)
KRS, Dacosta
PureHall
Dj Morpheus
(Free Zone - SSR)
Smos&BabyB
(Café d'Anvers - Fuse)
Clémentine, Bart
LIGHT AMBIANCE : HUGUES
PURE CLUB 23H-KRS > 2H30-J.SOMMERVILLE > 3H-BRANDY > 5H-DACOSTA ...
PURE HALL 23H-BART > 00H-SMOS&BABYB > 2H-MORPHEUS > 4H-CLÉMENTINE...
Dans la peau de
"Jimmy Sommerville"
Vous êtes dans les années 80, vous mesurez 1,65m, et vos tubes cartonnent dans les charts internationaux. L'espace d'un soir vous serez dans la peau de Jimmy Sommerville.
Pour y parvenir suivez cette petite note explicative :
1
Munissez-vous d'un élastique
2
Faire passer l'élastique dans les trous du masque de chaque côté
3
Positionnez le masque sur votre visage de la manière suivante
Afin de vérifier que l'illusion fonctionne, vous pouvez vous exercer à chanter devant votre glace ou devant un ami, ces trois titres phares de la carrière de Jimmy :
"...Youuuuu make me feeeel miiiighty reeeal..."
"...Tell me whyyyyyyy ?..."
"...Comment teu dire adiou ?..."
Vous êtes fin prêt pour le live !!!
Entrée 8
(AVEC CARTE DE MEMBRE)
Entrée 10
(SANS CARTE DE MEMBRE)
OUT SOON
Red Bull

Saturday 16. 02. 2002,
Pure, Tournai, 295 × 205 mm.

Saturday 2 March
Charles Siegling (Technasia)
Luke Solomon
: Pierre, T-Quest, Deg - : Smos & Baby Bee, St. Dic
Entrance: 22h till 23h : 2.50 € - after 23h : 10.00 €
Saturday 9 March
Stacey Pullen
Frederik
: Pierre, Deg - : St. Dic exclusive 6 hrs. set
Entrance: 22h till 23h : 2.50 € - after 23h : 10.00 €
Saturday 16 March
Monika Kruse
Les Craven
: Pierre, Deg, T-Quest - : St. Dic (Smos & Baby Bee will be playing at Arena/Amsterdam/Holland)
Entrance: 22h till 23h : 2.50 € - after 23h : 10.00 €
Saturday 23 March
Dave Clarke
Koenie
: Deg, T-Quest - : Smos & Baby Bee, St. Dic (Pierre will be playing at Spyce Club/Grenoble/France)
Entrance: 22h till 23h : 5.00 € - after 23h : 10.00 €
Saturday 30 March
DJ Rush
Hey you, sitting over there, you'd better get up, off your chair... Coz DJ Rush is coming to Fuse! Author of killer tunes such as Spitball, Freaks On Hubbard, Motherfucking Bass, the Shall We Dance LP and Clap Your Hands under his Russian Roulette moniker, but also a smashing DJ of course. Witness and believe!
: Pierre, Deg, T-Quest - : Smos & Baby Bee, St. Dic
Entrance: 22h till 23h : 2.50 € - after 23h : 10.00 €
fuse
motion

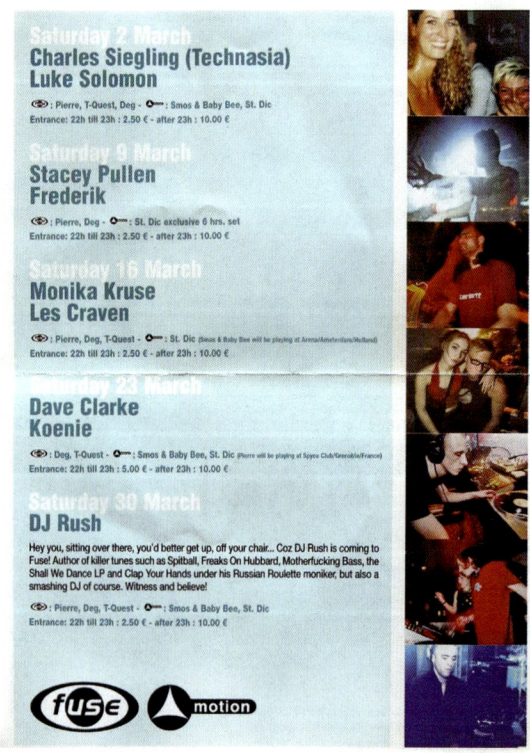

March 2002, Fuse,
Brussels, 140 × 95 mm.

Sunday 17. 03. 2002, Zoo , Pecq, 150 × 120 mm.

May & June 2002, *Food*
at Lounge Club, Brussels, 210 × 150 mm.

April 2002, Culture Club & SMAK,
Ghent, 340 × 120 mm.

Saturday 20. 04. 2002, *Stuurboord*
at Hangar 26/27, Antwerp, 150 × 150 mm.

Tuesday 30. 04. 2002, *Bel Mondo*
at SMAK, Ghent, 340 × 120 mm.

May & June 2002, *Food*
at Lounge Club, Brussels, 210 × 150 mm.

Sunday 17. 03. 2002, *Zoo*, Pecq, 150 × 120 mm.

April 2002, Culture Club & SMAK,
Ghent, 340 × 120 mm.

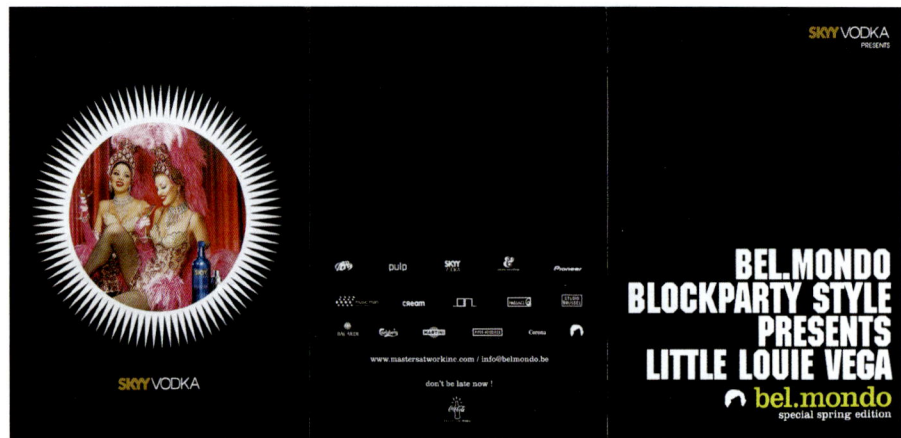

Tuesday 30. 04. 2002, *Bel Mondo*
at SMAK, Ghent, 340 × 120 mm.

Saturday 20. 04. 2002, *Stuurboord*
at Hangar 26/27, Antwerp, 150 × 150 mm.

May 2002, Fuse,
Brussels, 140 × 95 mm.

June 2002, Fuse,
Brussels, 140 × 95 mm.

April 2002, Fuse,
Brussels, 140 × 95 mm.

Saturday 15. 06. 2002, Lounge,
Charleroi, 125 × 125 mm.

June 2002, Fuse,
Brussels, 140 × 95 mm.

May 2002, Fuse,
Brussels, 140 × 95 mm.

April 2002, Fuse,
Brussels, 140 × 95 mm.

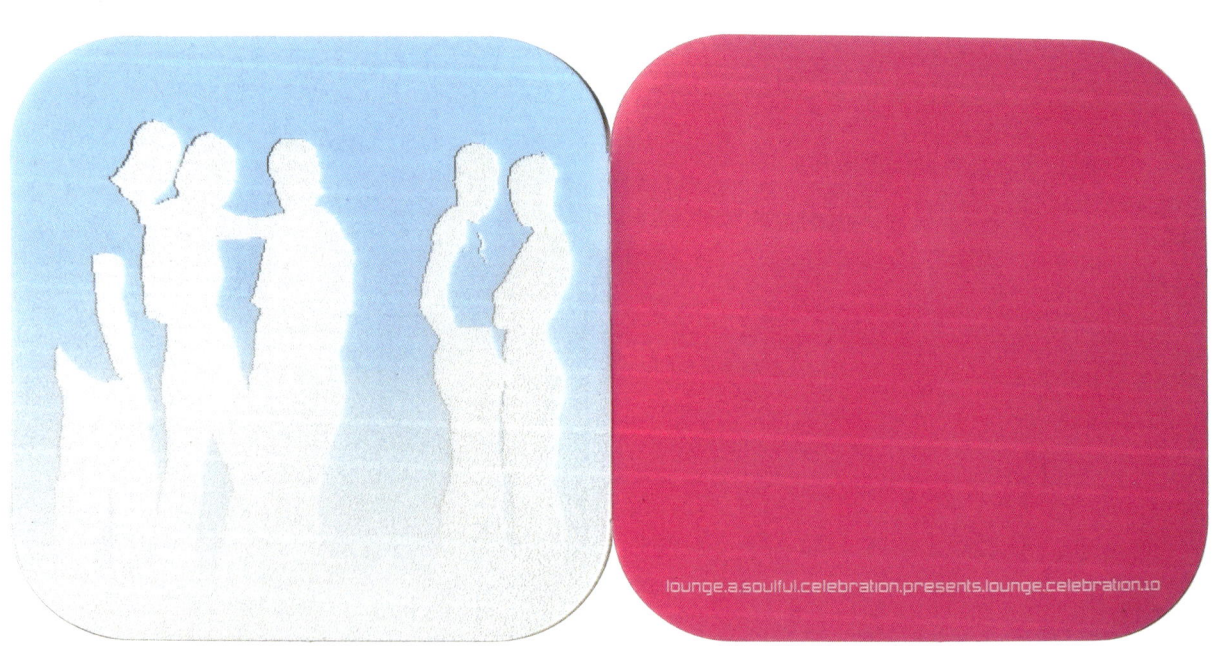

Saturday 15. 06. 2002, Lounge,
Charleroi, 125 × 125 mm.

July 2002, 10 days off, Ghent, 290 × 290 mm.

Saturday 15. 06. 2002, Lounge,
Charleroi, 125 × 125 mm.

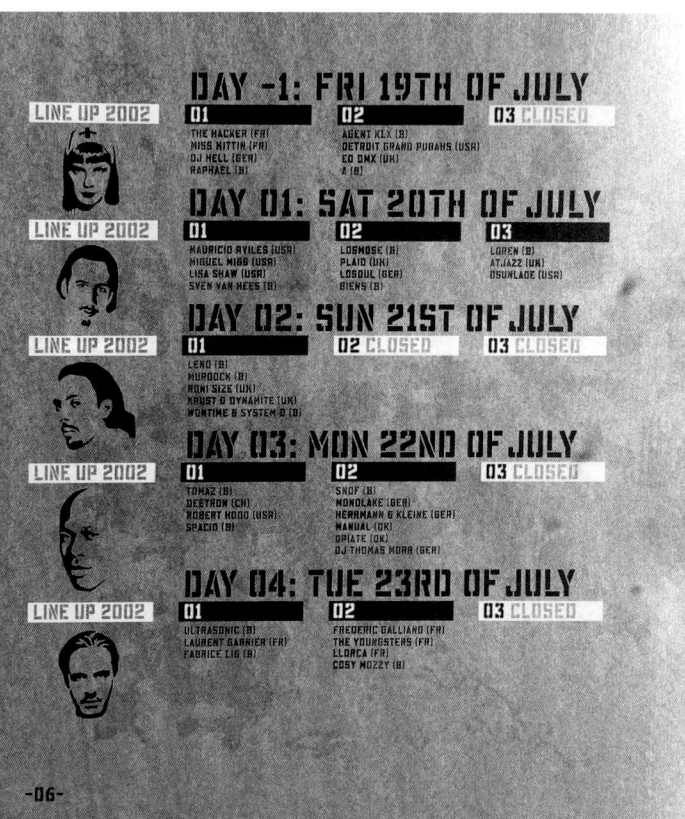

July 2002, 10 days off, Ghent, 290 × 290 mm.

Summer 2002, Fuse,
Brussels, 140 × 95 mm.

Friday 08. 03. 2002, Musical Maturity,
Ciney, 143 × 105 mm.

July 2002, House Torhout, Torhout, 420 × 295 mm.

Friday 08. 03. 2002, Musical Maturity,
Ciney, 143 × 105 mm.

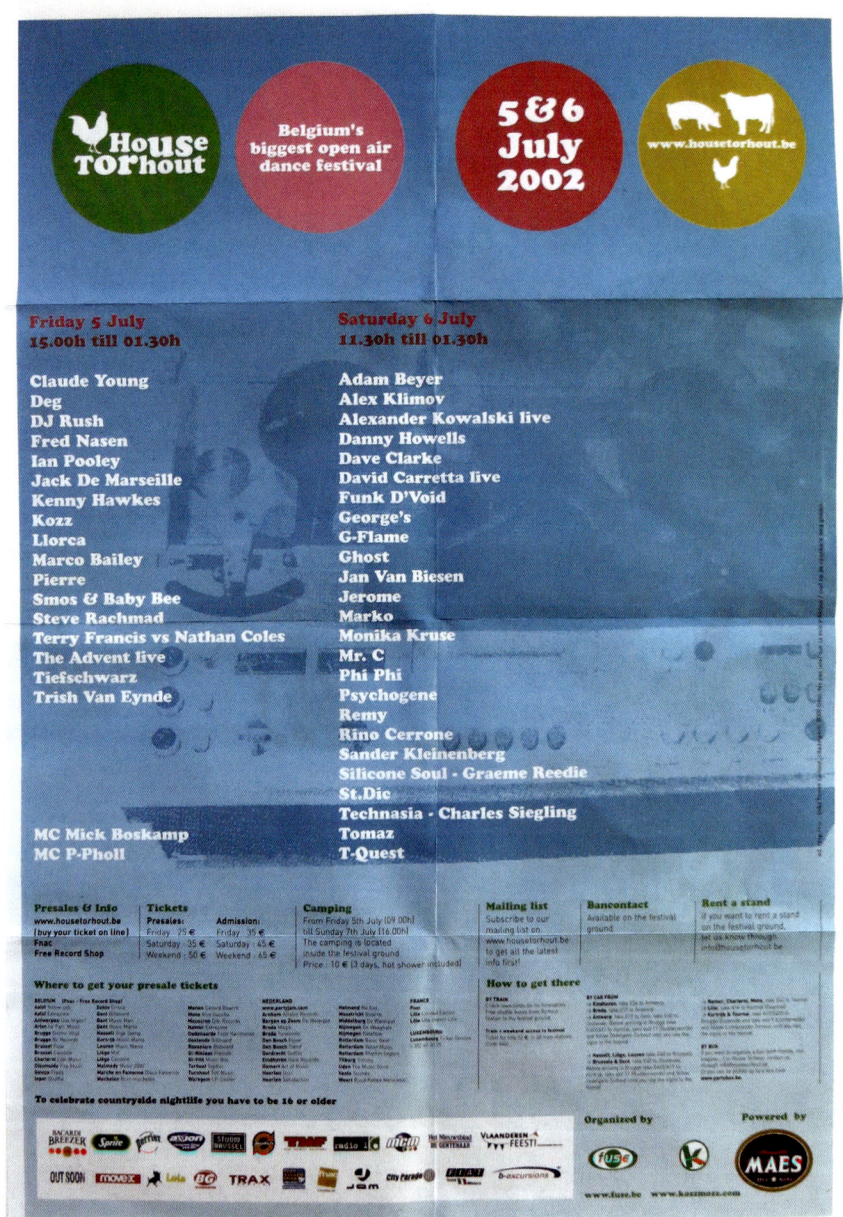

July 2002, House Torhout, Torhout, 420 × 295 mm.

Summer 2002, Fuse,
Brussels, 140 × 95 mm.

Wednesday 14. 08. 2002, *Fuse On The Beach* at
Ostend Beach & Casino, Ostend, 210 × 150 mm.

Wednesday 14. 08. 2002, *Fuse On The Beach* at Ostend Beach & Casino, Ostend, 210 × 150 mm.

September 2002, Fill Collins Club, Antwerp, 210 × 150 mm.

September 2002, Fuse, Brussels, 140 × 95 mm.

September 2002, Café Capital, Antwerp, 123 × 123 mm.

Saturday 14. 09. 2002, Laundry Day, Antwerp, 210 × 150 mm.

September 2002, Café Capital, Antwerp, 123 × 123 mm.

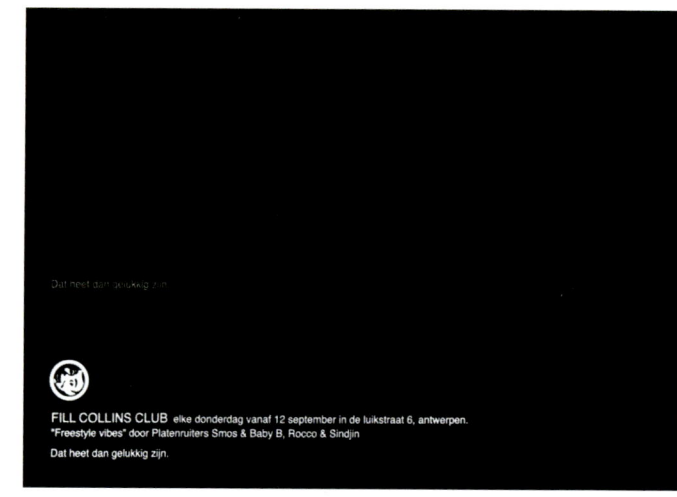

September 2002, Fill Collins Club, Antwerp, 210 × 150 mm.

September 2002, Fuse, Brussels, 140 × 95 mm.

Saturday 14. 09. 2002, Laundry Day, Antwerp, 210 × 150 mm.

October 2002, F.C. Geluk, Antwerp, 150 × 105 mm.

October 2002, Fuse, Brussels, 140 × 95 mm.

November 2002,
Fuse, Brussels, 150 × 105 mm.

October 2002, *Food*
at Lounge Club, Brussels, 210 × 150 mm.

October 2002, Fuse, Brussels, 140 × 95 mm.

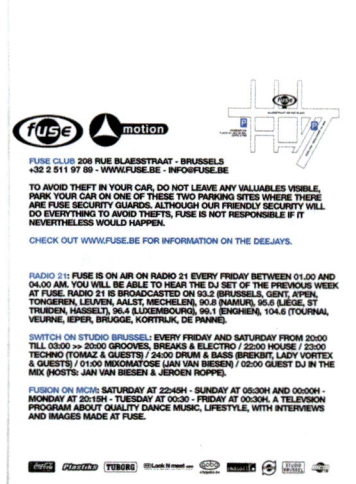

November 2002,
Fuse, Brussels, 150 × 105 mm.

October 2002, *Food*
at Lounge Club, Brussels, 210 × 150 mm.

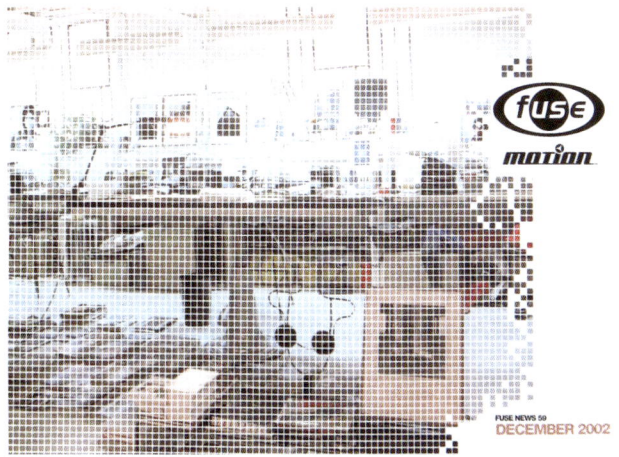

December 2002,
Fuse, Brussels, 150 × 105 mm.

October & November 2002,
Fataal at Musicafé, Leuven, 150 × 105 mm.

Friday 15. 11. 2002,
Café d'Anvers, Antwerp, 210 × 100 mm.

October 2002, Café d'Anvers,
Antwerp, 120 × 83 mm.

December 2002,
Fuse, Brussels, 150 × 105 mm.

Friday 15. 11. 2002,
Café d'Anvers, Antwerp, 210 × 100 mm.

October & November 2002,
Fataal at Musicafé, Leuven, 150 × 105 mm.

October 2002, Café d'Anvers,
Antwerp, 120 × 83 mm.

October 2002, *Food*
at Lounge Club, Brussels, 210 × 150 mm.

December 2002, Pure, Tournai, 213 × 160 mm.

December 2002, Café d'Anvers,
Antwerp, 120 × 83 mm.

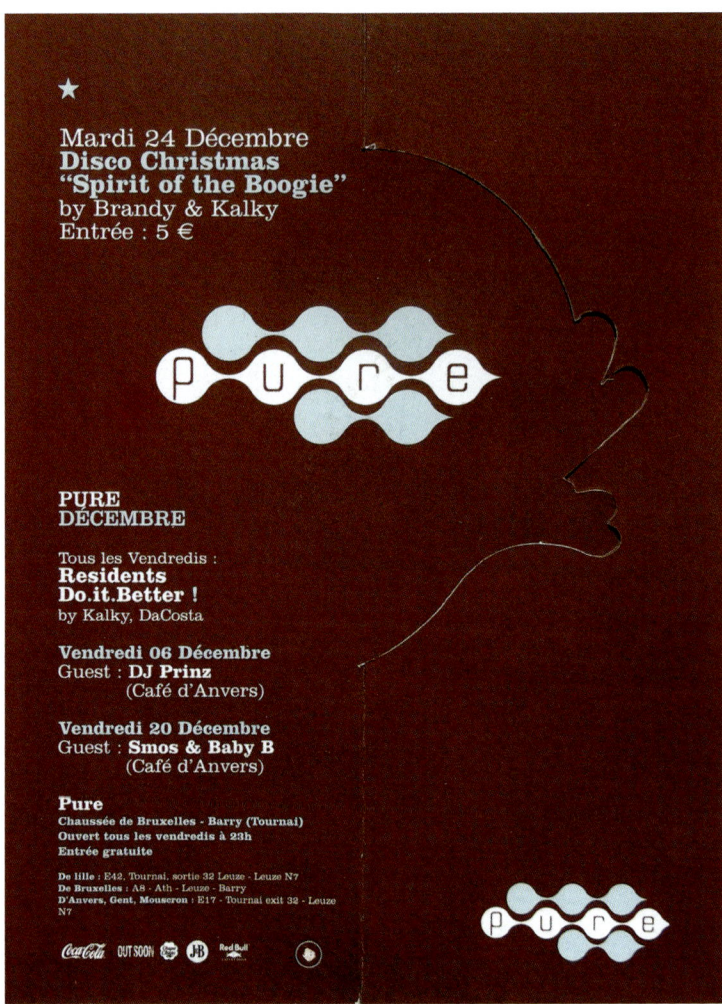 

December 2002, Pure, Tournai, 213 × 160 mm.

December 2002, Café d'Anvers,
Antwerp, 120 × 83 mm.

February 2003, Café d'Anvers,
Antwerp, 120 × 84 mm.

March 2003, Café d'Anvers,
Antwerp, 120 × 84 mm.

January 2003, Fuse,
Brussels, 300 × 102 mm.

February 2003, Fuse,
Brussels, 300 × 102 mm.

March 2003,
Café d'Anvers, Antwerp, 120 × 84 mm.

February 2003,
Café d'Anvers, Antwerp, 120 × 84 mm.

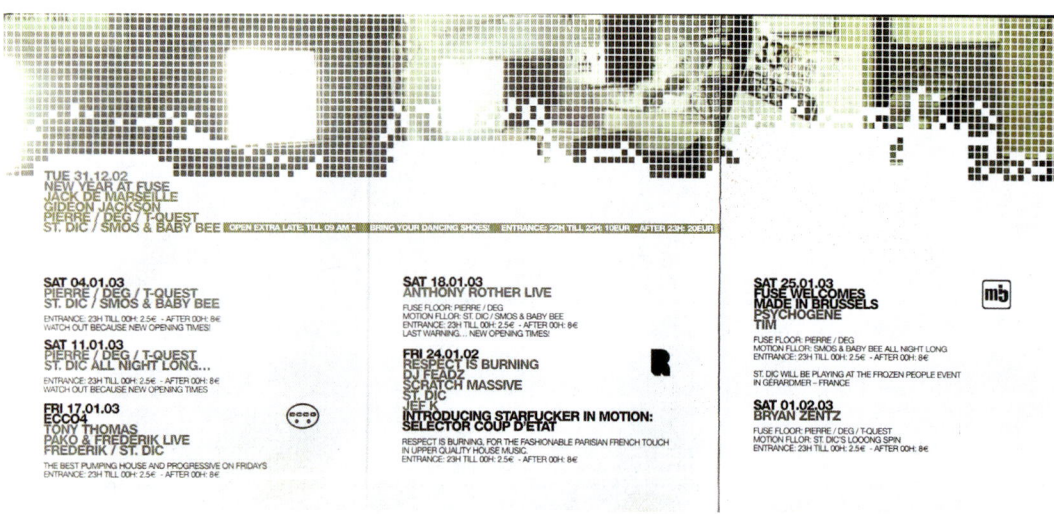

January 2003, Fuse,
Brussels, 300 × 102 mm.

February 2003, Fuse,
Brussels, 300 × 102 mm.

March 2003, Fuse,
Brussels, 300 × 102 mm.

March 2003, Decadence, Ghent, 220 × 100 mm.

Wednesday 30. 04. 2003,
E-motionz at Silo, Leuven, 215 × 150 mm.

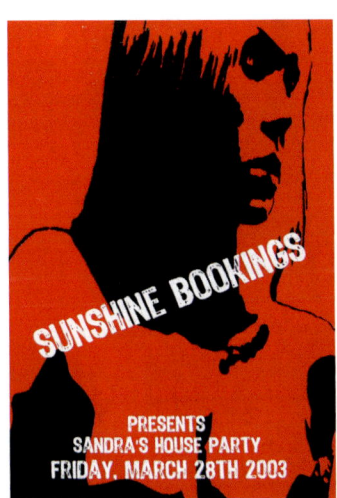

Friday 28. 03. 2003, *Sunshine Bookings presents Sandra's House Party* at Decandence, Ghent, 150 × 105 mm.

Saturday 03. 05. 2003, *Elle et moi* at Club Geluk, Antwerp, 150 × 105 mm.

March 2003, Fuse,
Brussels, 300 × 102 mm.

Wednesday 30. 04. 2003,
E-motionz at Silo, Leuven, 215 × 150 mm.

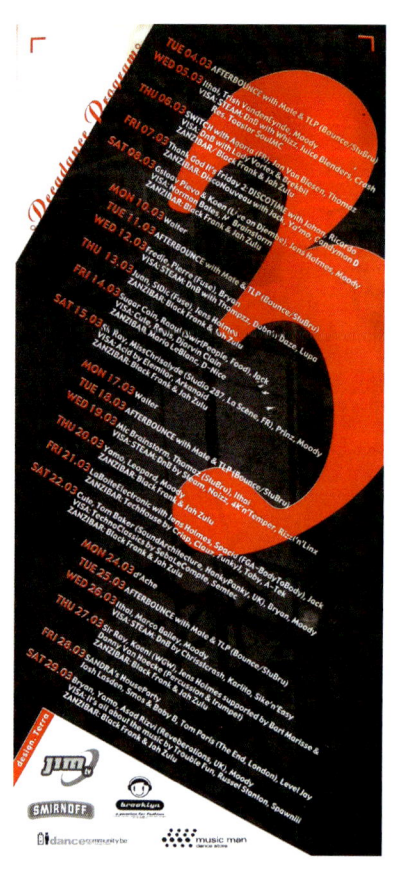

March 2003, Decadence, Ghent, 220 × 100 mm.

Saturday 03. 05. 2003, *Elle et moi* at Club Geluk, Antwerp, 150 × 105 mm.

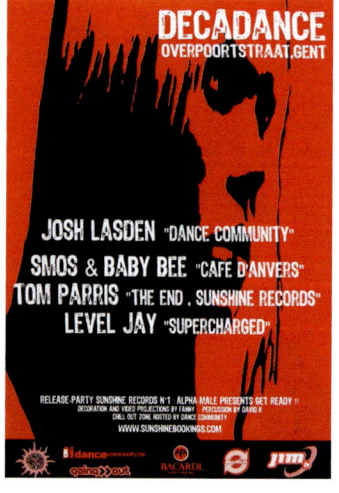

Friday 28. 03. 2003, *Sunshine Bookings presents Sandra's House Party* at Decadence, Ghent, 150 × 105 mm.

May 2003, Fuse, Brussels,
300 × 102 mm.

April 2003, Café d'Anvers,
Antwerp, 120 × 84 mm.

May 2003, Café d'Anvers,
Antwerp, 120 × 84 mm.

April & May 2003, Decadence,
Ghent, 220 × 100 mm.

Friday 04. 04. 2003, *Ravin* at Café d'Anvers,
Antwerp, 280 × 210 mm.

May 2003, Fuse, Brussels, 300 × 102 mm.

May 2003, Café d'Anvers, Antwerp, 120 × 84 mm.

April 2003, Café d'Anvers, Antwerp, 120 × 84 mm.

Friday 04. 04. 2003, *Ravin* at Café d'Anvers, Antwerp, 280 × 210 mm.

April & May 2003, Decadence, Ghent, 220 × 100 mm.

Friday 04. 07. 2003, *Rhythmanin'*
at Kaaiman, Antwerp, 150 × 105 mm.

Friday 25. 07. 2003,
Pravda House Nights
at Decandence, Ghent, ⌀ 143 mm.

June. 2003, Café d'Anvers, Antwerp, 210 × 95 mm.

Saturday 28. 06. 2003,
Plug One at Fuse, Brussels, 215 × 150 mm.

June 2003, Fuse,
Brussels, 300 × 102 mm.

Friday 25. 07. 2003,
Pravda House Nights
at Decandence, Ghent, ⌀ 143 mm.

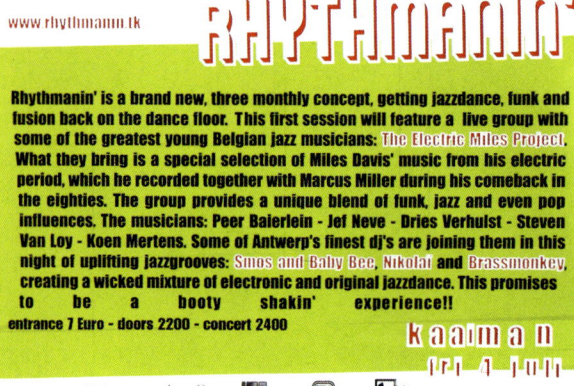

Friday 04. 07. 2003, *Rhythmanin'*
at Kaaiman, Antwerp, 150 × 105 mm.

June. 2003, Café d'Anvers, Antwerp, 210 × 95 mm.

Saturday 28. 06. 2003,
Plug One at Fuse,
Brussels, 215 × 150 mm.

June 2003, Fuse,
Brussels, 300 × 102 mm.

Summer 2003, Fuse,
Brussels, 300 × 102 mm.

Saturday 23. 08. 2003, Pure, Barry, 200 × 77 mm.

August 2003, Café Capital,
Antwerp, 150 × 105 mm.

August 2003, FestiVibe,
Thuillies, 210 × 95 mm.

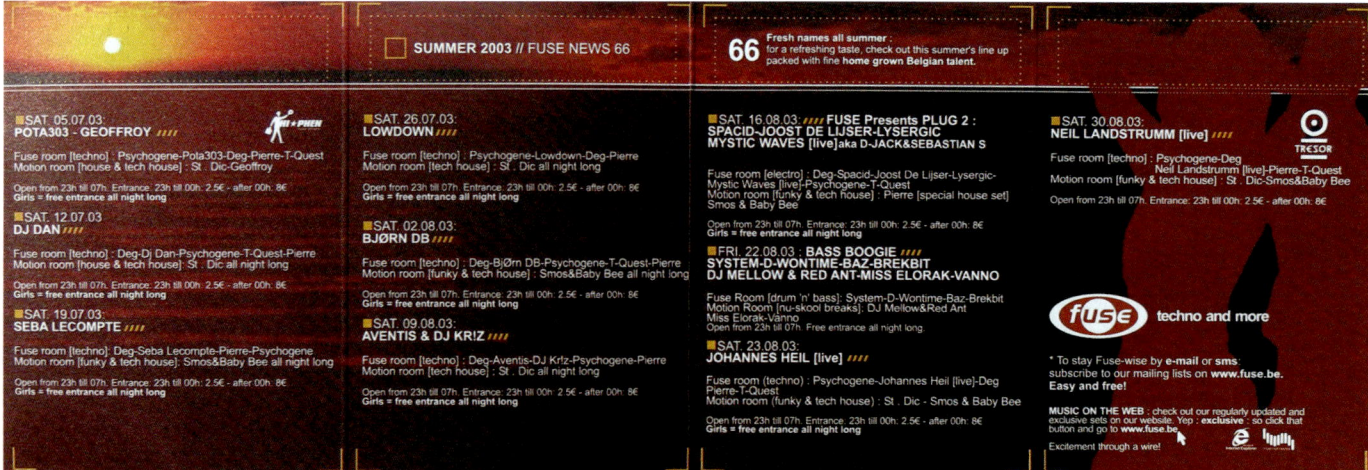

Summer 2003, Fuse,
Brussels, 300 × 102 mm.

August 2003, Café Capital,
Antwerp, 150 × 105 mm.

August 2003, FestiVibe,
Thuillies, 210 × 95 mm.

Saturday 23. 08. 2003, Pure, Barry, 200 × 77 mm.

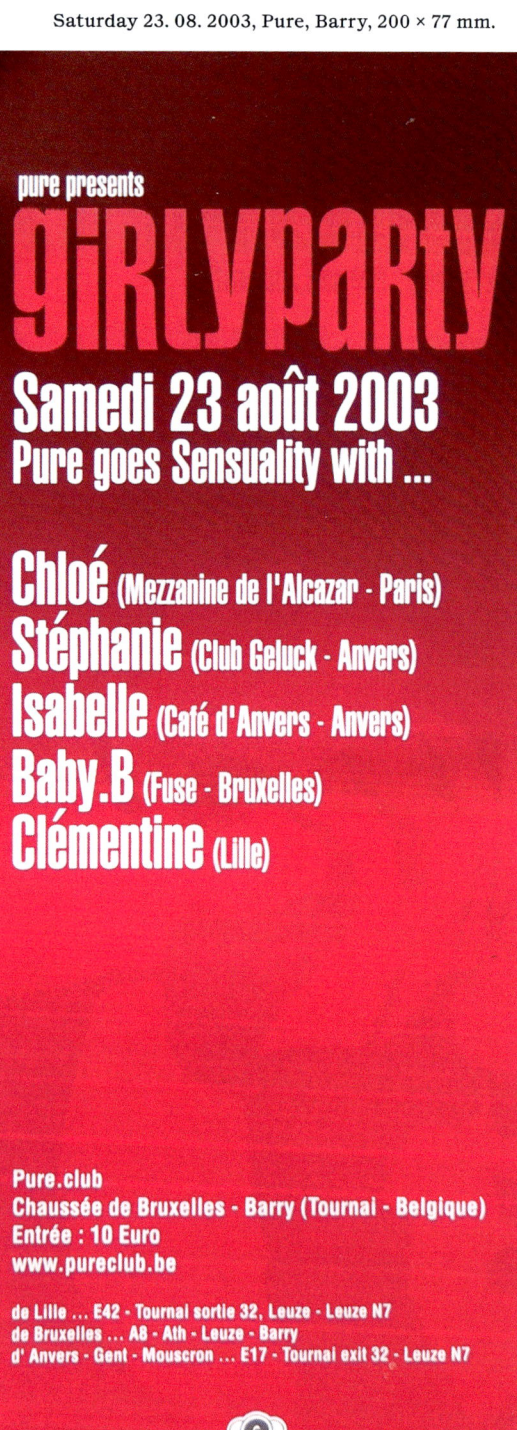

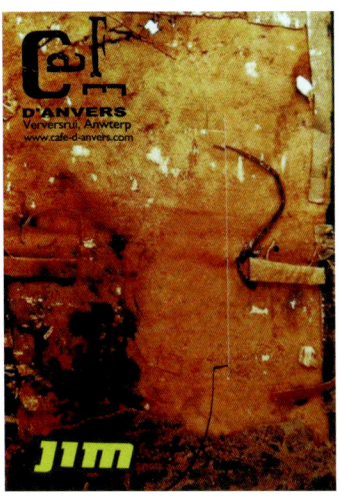

October 2003, Café d'Anvers,
Antwerp, 120 × 84 mm.

Autumn 2003, Fuse, Brussels, 300 × 102 mm.

Friday 28. 11. 2003, *Flavourz* at Club Govio,
Kalmthout, 150 × 105 mm.

Friday 10. 10. 2003, *E-Motionz*
at Silo, Leuven, 150 × 105 mm.

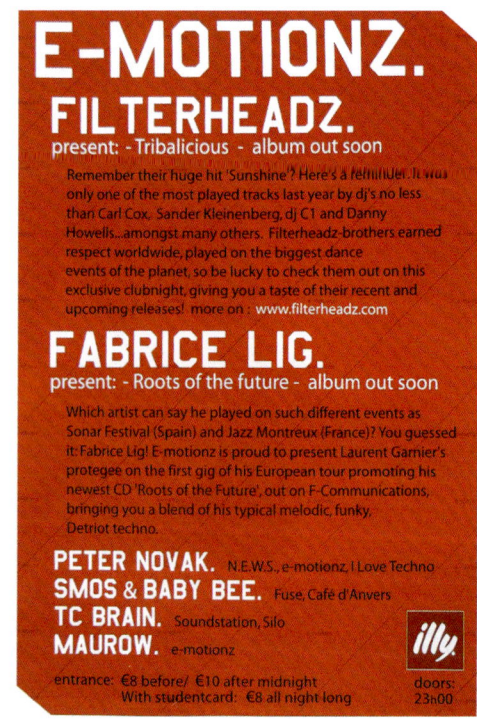

Friday 10. 10. 2003, *E-Motionz*
at Silo, Leuven, 150 × 105 mm.

Friday 28. 11. 2003, *Flavourz* at Club Govio,
Kalmthout, 150 × 105 mm.

October 2003, Café d'Anvers, Antwerp, 120 × 84 mm.

Saturday 04. 10. 2003, *Touch Parties: Frequencies* at Club 9, Koersel, 215 × 150 mm.

Saturday 01. 11. 2003, *Sensuality* at H₂O Club, Pecq, 210 × 150 mm.

Saturday 20. 12. 2003, *Sub Club* at Pure, Antwerp, 210 × 95 mm.

Saturday 04. 10. 2003, *Touch Parties: Frequencies* at Club 9, Koersel, 215 × 150 mm.

Saturday 01. 11. 2003, *Sensuality* at H₂O Club, Pecq, 210 × 150 mm.

Saturday 20. 12. 2003, *Sub Club* at Pure, Antwerp, 210 × 95 mm.

2004, *Saturdays Resident Night* at Café d'Anvers, Antwerp, 147 × 102 mm.

Saturday 28. 02. 2004, Music Please, Namur, 147 × 102 mm.

January 2004, Fuse, Brussels, 300 × 102 mm.

February & March 2004, Tijuana, Ghent, 210 × 100 mm.

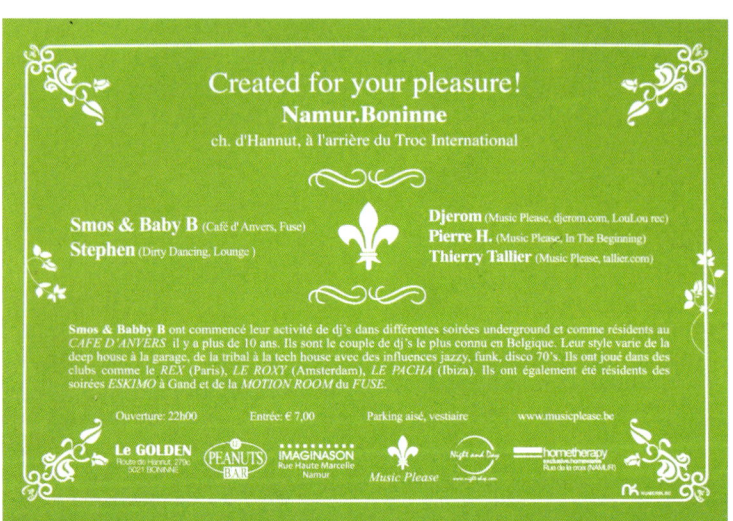

Saturday 28. 02. 2004,
Music Please, Namur, 147 × 102 mm.

2004, *Saturdays Resident Night*
at Café d'Anvers, Antwerp, 147 × 102 mm.

January 2004, Fuse,
Brussels, 300 × 102 mm.

February & March 2004,
Tijuana, Ghent, 210 × 100 mm.

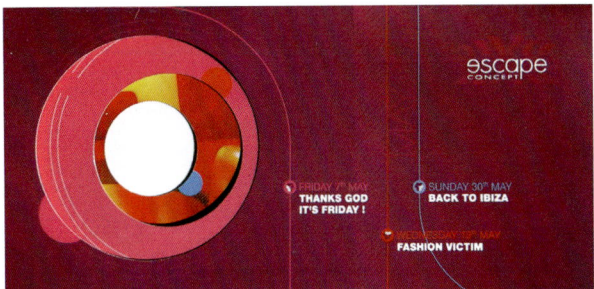

May 2004, Escape Concept,
Warcoing, 300 × 210 mm.

May 2004, Tijuana,
Ghent, 210 × 100 mm.

Friday 05. 03. 2004, *Eskimo*
at Eskimo Factory, Ghent, 595 × 420 mm.

August 2004, Café Capital,
Antwerp, 210 × 100 mm.

May 2004, Tijuana,
Ghent, 210 × 100 mm.

May 2004, Escape Concept,
Warcoing, 300 × 210 mm.

August 2004, Café Capital,
Antwerp, 210 × 100 mm.

Friday 05. 03. 2004, *Eskimo*
at Eskimo Factory, Ghent, 595 × 420 mm.

June & July 2004, Tijuana, Ghent, 210 × 100 mm.

Friday 02. 07. 2004, *Les Demoiselles* at Tavernier, Brussels, ⌀ 120 mm.

Friday 12. 11. 2004, *Designers Against Aids* at Café d'Anvers, Antwerp, 147 × 102 mm.

Saturday 27. 11. 2004, *Play* at Café Capital, Antwerp, 147 × 102 mm.

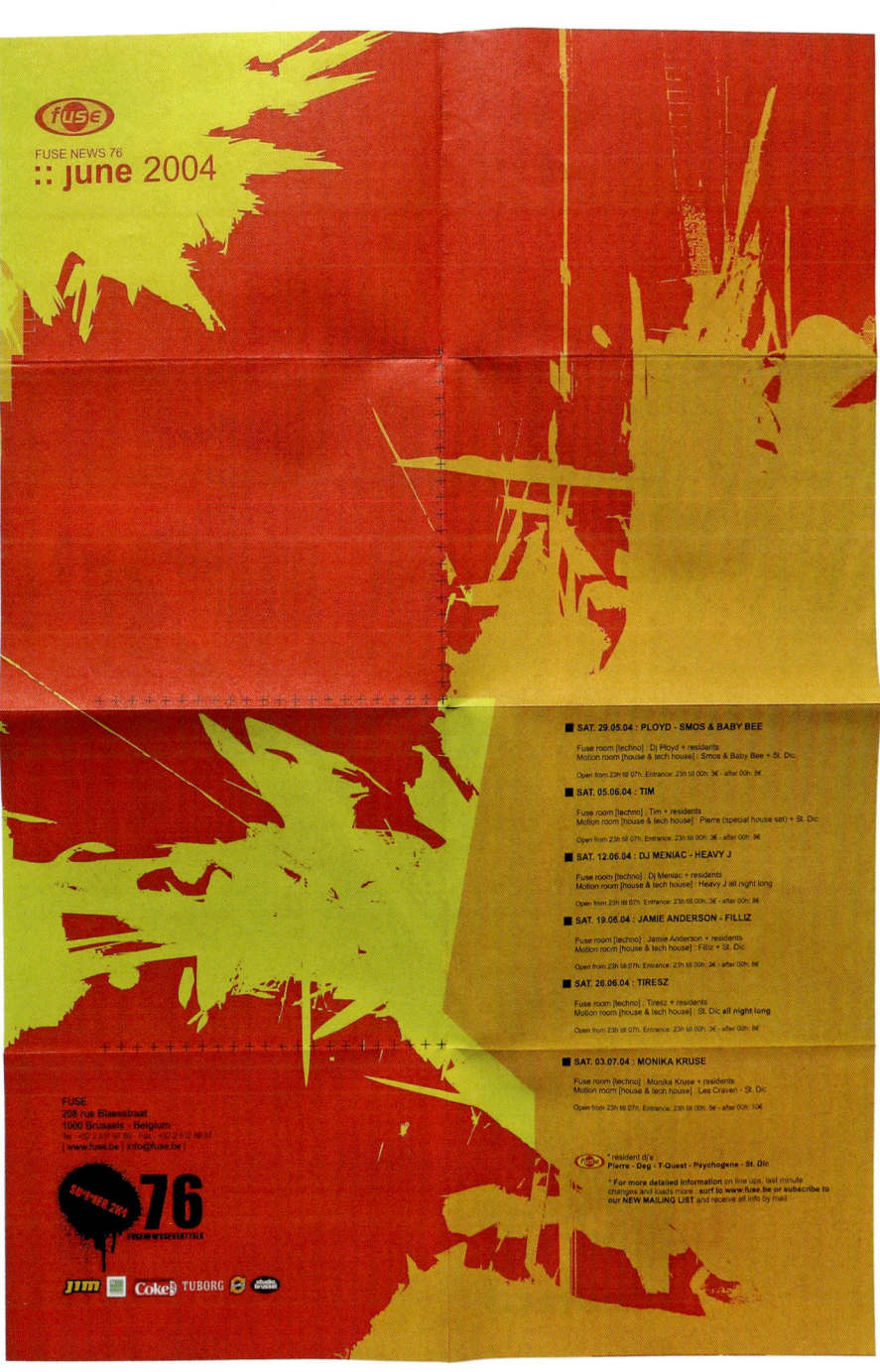

May, June & July. 2004, Fuse, Brussels, 415 × 294 mm.

Friday 02. 07. 2004, *Les Demoiselles* at Tavernier, Brussels, ⌀ 120 mm.

June & July 2004, Tijuana, Ghent, 210 × 100 mm.

Friday 12. 11. 2004, *Designers Against Aids* at Café d'Anvers, Antwerp, 147 × 102 mm.

Saturday 27. 11. 2004, *Play* at Café Capital, Antwerp, 147 × 102 mm.

July & August. 2004, Fuse, Brussels, 415 × 294 mm.

July & August 2004, Petrol, Antwerp, 120 × 120 mm.

May 2004, *Flower Power*
at Barocco, Tongeren, 296 × 207 mm.

July 2004, *Ghent by night* at Lodge Van Eyck
Swimming Pool, Ghent, 298 × 102 mm.

Monday 05. 07. 2004, *Sesiones de Funktec
Esperanza* at Lazzurra, Maaseik, 147 × 102 mm.

Saturday 24. 04. 2004, *Break Down*
at Muziekodroom, Hasselt, 210 × 147 mm.

May 2004, *Flower Power*
at Barocco, Tongeren, 296 × 207 mm.

July 2004, *Ghent by night* at Lodge Van Eyck
Swimming Pool, Ghent, 298 × 102 mm.

Saturday 24. 04. 2004, *Break Down*
at Muziekodroom, Hasselt, 210 × 147 mm.

Monday 05. 07. 2004, *Sesiones de Funktec
Esperanza* at Lazzurra, Maaseik, 147 × 102 mm.

ZATERDAG 14 AUGUSTUS (DEUREN 23u)
23u: MÄRTINI BRÖS (D), HERMANOS INGLESOS, JOSZ LE BON, LOUIS KATORZ

DONDERDAG 19 AUGUSTUS (DEUREN 21u)
22u: SUITE VOOR SPREEKSTEM, HOMMAGE GUST GILS MET PETER VAN DE VEIRE, SPINVIS (NL), DIDI DE PARIS, TOM NAEGELS, HANS PLOMP (NL), JULES DEELDER (NL) EN MARCEL VANTHILT
23u: THE WHODADS, DJ JULES DEELDER (NL) EN OLE SOLLIED

VRIJDAG 20 AUGUSTUS (DEUREN 21u)
22u: CLAUS ATTACK MET ABSYNTHE MINDED, GROEP JEZUS EN GRIM
23u: MOODLEX XL, DJ T (D), ELASTIX

ZATERDAG 21 AUGUSTUS (DEUREN 23u)
23u: SEX IN DALLAS (D), COSY MOZZY, JOSZ LE BON, LOUIS KATORZ

DONDERDAG 26 AUGUSTUS (DEUREN 21u)
22u: HET ZOMERT IN BARAKSTAD / HOMMAGE JMH BERCKMANS ROLAND, PJERO ROOBJEE, STIJN MEURIS, PETER VAN DEN EEDE TOM LANOYE, LUC DE VOS, ELVIS PEETERS, ELKE DOM, VITALSKI
23u: DJ'S ARE NOT ROCKSTARS (PRINCESS SUPERSTAR + ALEXANDER TECHNIQUE) (VS), MAURO, SULTANZ OF ZZWING

VRIJDAG 27 AUGUSTUS (DEUREN 21u)
22u: SONGLINES MET JOHN S.HALL (VS, KING MISSILE), THÉ LAU (NL), STIJN
23u: STIJN, MASKESMACHINE, ROOTY (GB), PIPCO

ZATERDAG 28 AUGUSTUS (DEUREN 23u)
23u: BRISKEY, K-BONUS, JOSZ LE BON, LOUIS KATORZ

July & August 2004, Petrol, Antwerp, 120 × 120 mm.

Saturday 26. 06. 2004,
City Parade, Ghent, 250 × 145 mm.

May 2004, Billion Club,
Gourain Romecroix, 210 × 100 mm.

October 2004, *15 years CDA* at Café d'Anvers,
Antwerp, 100 × 100 mm.

15 YEARS CAFE D'ANVERS

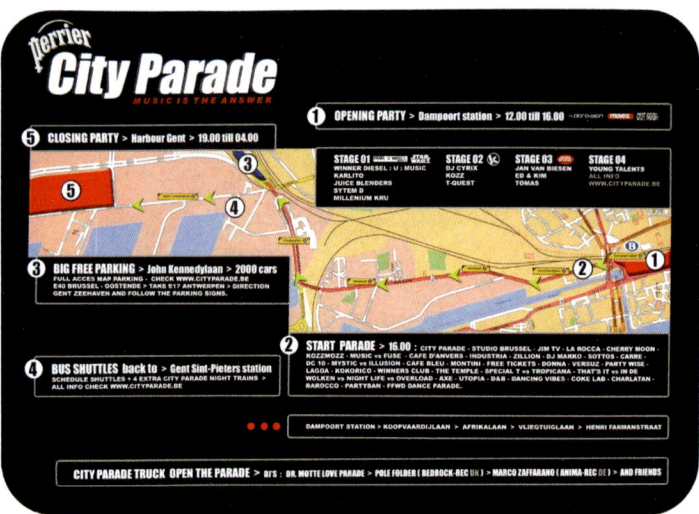

Saturday 26. 06. 2004,
City Parade, Ghent, 250 × 145 mm.

July & August 2004, Petrol, Antwerp, 120 × 120 mm.

May 2004, Billion Club,
Gourain Romecroix, 210 × 100 mm.

October 2004, *15 years CDA* at Café d'Anvers, Antwerp, 100 × 100 mm.

Saturday 19. 02. 2005, *Dirty Dancing* at Mirano, Brussels, 210 × 150 mm.

Friday 24. 06. 2005, *Hed Kandi presents: Back to love* at That Factory, Ghent, 150 × 105 mm.

January 2005, Milk Club, Brussels, 205 × 145 mm.

February, March & April 2005, Fuse, Brussels, 295 × 420 mm.

Friday 24. 06. 2005, *Hed Kandi presents: Back to love* at That Factory, Ghent, 150 × 105 mm.

Saturday 19. 02. 2005, *Dirty Dancing* at Mirano, Brussels, 210 × 150 mm.

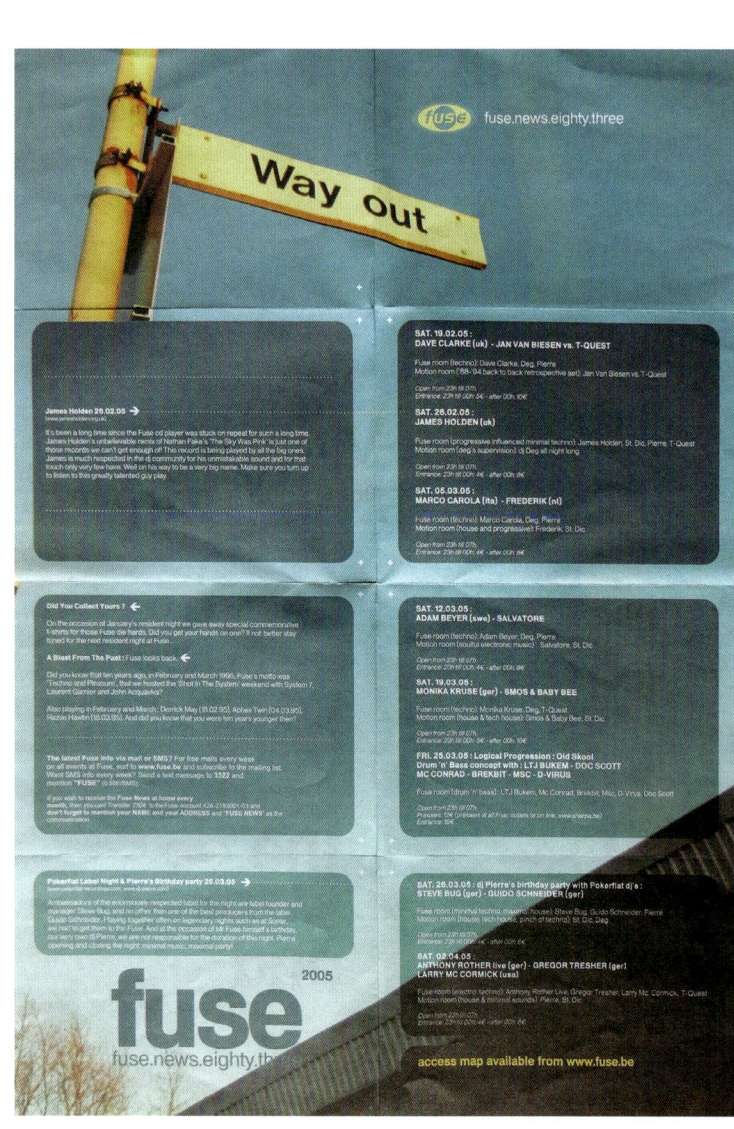

February, March & April 2005, Fuse, Brussels, 295 × 420 mm.

January 2005, Milk Club, Brussels, 205 × 145 mm.

October 2005, *16 years CDA* at Café d'Anvers, Antwerp, 298 × 105 mm.

Autumn & Winter. 2005, VIP Club, Mons, 275 × 130 mm.

Saturday 31. 12. 2005, *New Year In Camouflage* at Café d'Anvers, Antwerp, 200 × 200 mm.

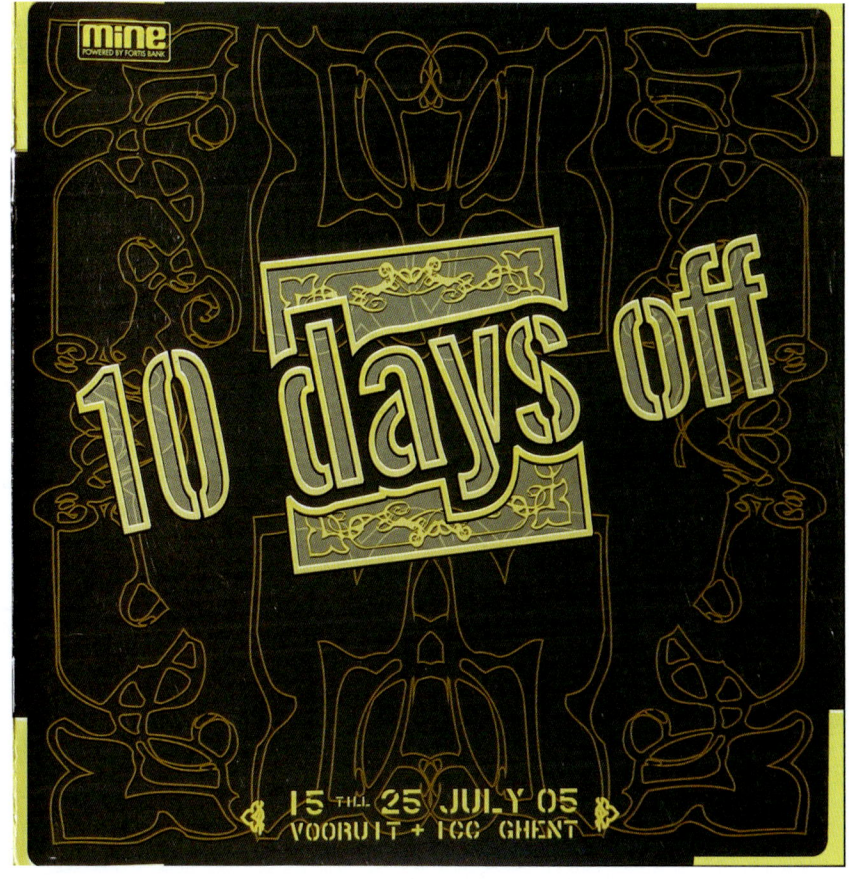

15.–25. 05. 2005, 10 days off, Ghent, 200 × 200 mm.

2005

147

October 2005, *16 years CDA* at Café d'Anvers, Antwerp, 298 × 105 mm.

Saturday 31. 12. 2005, *New Year In Camouflage* at Café d'Anvers, Antwerp, 200 × 200 mm.

Autumn & Winter. 2005, VIP Club, Mons, 275 × 130 mm.

15.–25. 05. 2005, 10 days off, Ghent, 200 × 200 mm.

Sunday 14. 08. 2005, *A divine sunday* at Château de Sombreffe, Sombreffe, 150 × 120 mm.

October & November 2005,
Fuse, Brussels, 295 × 420 mm.

November 2005, BLISS,
La Glanerie, 290 × 100 mm.

November 2005, BLISS,
La Glanerie, 290 × 100 mm.

Sunday 14. 08. 2005, *A divine sunday* at Château de Sombreffe, Sombreffe, 150 × 120 mm.

October & November 2005,
Fuse, Brussels, 295 × 420 mm.

Sunday 14. 08. 2005, Tomorrowland, Boom, 840 × 590 mm.

Saturday 03. 09. 2005, Laundry Day, Antwerp, 150 × 105 mm.

Saturday 08. 10. 2005, *Classics* at Café d'Anvers, Antwerp, 150 × 105 mm.

Saturday 20. 08. 2005, *Punk'id* at Charlatan, Ghent, 100 × 100 mm.

2005

Sunday 14. 08. 2005, Tomorrowland, Boom, 840 × 590 mm.

Saturday 20. 08. 2005, *Punk'id* at Charlatan, Ghent, 100 × 100 mm.

Saturday 08. 10. 2005, *Classics* at Café d'Anvers, Antwerp, 150 × 105 mm.

Saturday 15. 07. 2006,
Fake Bar, Antwerp, 150 × 105 mm.

February & March 2006,
Fuse, Brussels, 420 × 295 mm.

Friday 14. 04. 2006, *Flashback* at Café d'Anvers,
Antwerp, 298 × 210 mm.

Saturday 15. 07. 2006,
Fake Bar, Antwerp, 150 × 105 mm.

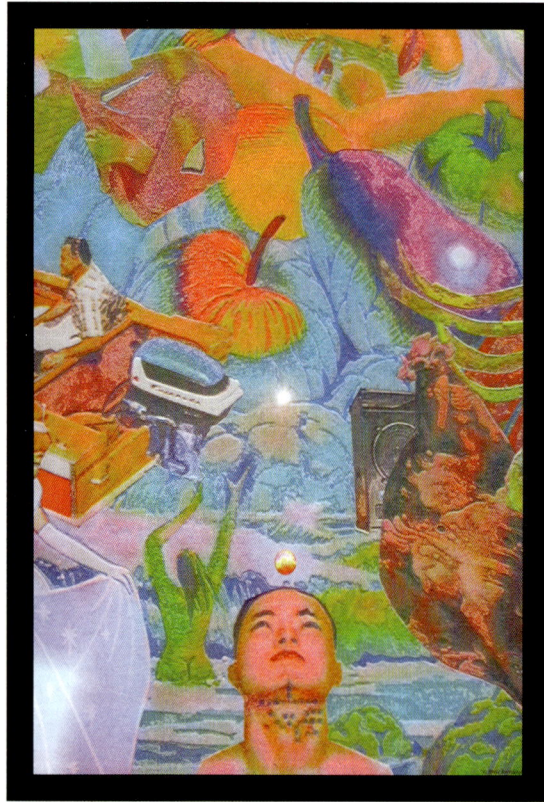

Friday 14. 04. 2006, *Flashback* at Café d'Anvers,
Antwerp, 298 × 210 mm.

February & March 2006,
Fuse, Brussels, 420 × 295 mm.

July & August 2006, *Breakdown Summer Residency* at Muziekodroom, Hasselt, 150 × 105 mm.

Thursday 20. 07. 2006, *Duo Night* at Music Please, Namur, 150 × 105 mm.

Sunday 30. 07. 2006, Tomorrowland, Boom, 240 × 120 mm.

April & May 2006, Petrol, Antwerp, 120 × 120 mm.

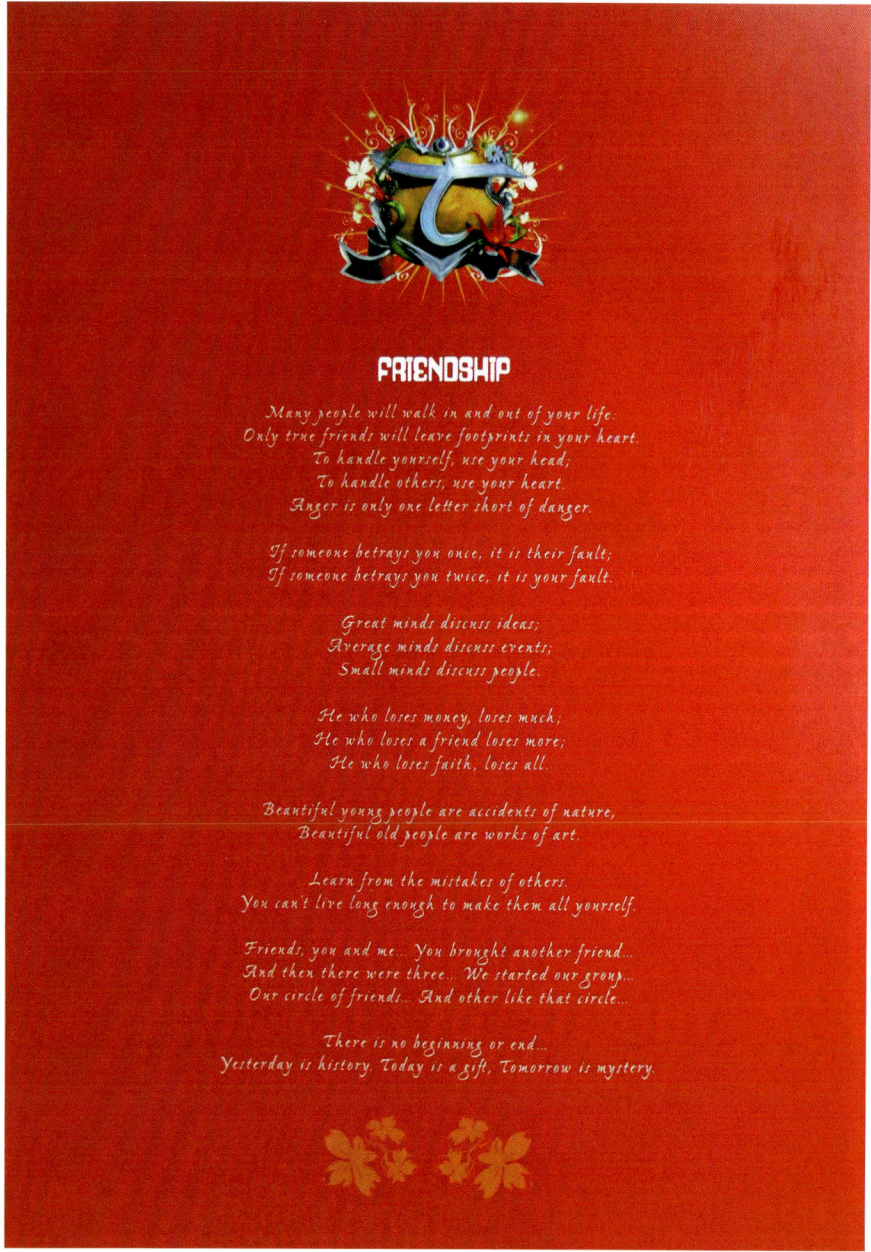

Sunday 30. 07. 2006, Tomorrowland,
Boom, 240 × 120 mm.

July & August 2006, *Breakdown
Summer Residency* at Muziekodroom,
Hasselt, 150 × 105 mm.

Thursday 20. 07. 2006, *Duo Night*
at Music Please, Namur, 150 × 105 mm.

April & May 2006, Petrol,
Antwerp, 120 × 120 mm.

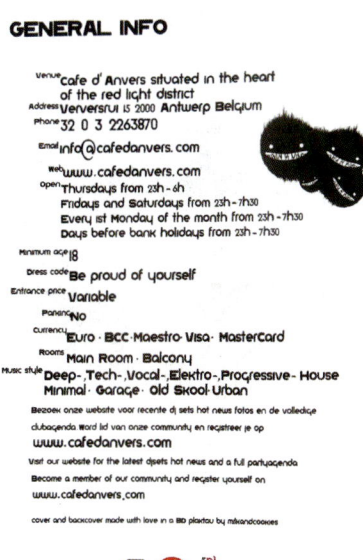

October 2006, *17 years CDA* at Café d'Anvers, Antwerp, 145 × 105 mm.

Friday 11. 08. 2006, the BLOCK PARTY, Sint-Truiden, 150 × 105 mm.

Saturday 25. 11. 2006, *Jockey Club* at l'Hippodrome de Wallonie, Mons, 200 × 108 mm.

October 2006, *17 years CDA* at Café d'Anvers, Antwerp, 145 × 105 mm.

Friday 11. 08. 2006, the BLOCK PARTY,
Sint-Truiden, 150 × 105 mm.

October 2006, *17 years CDA* at Café d'Anvers,
Antwerp, 145 × 105 mm.

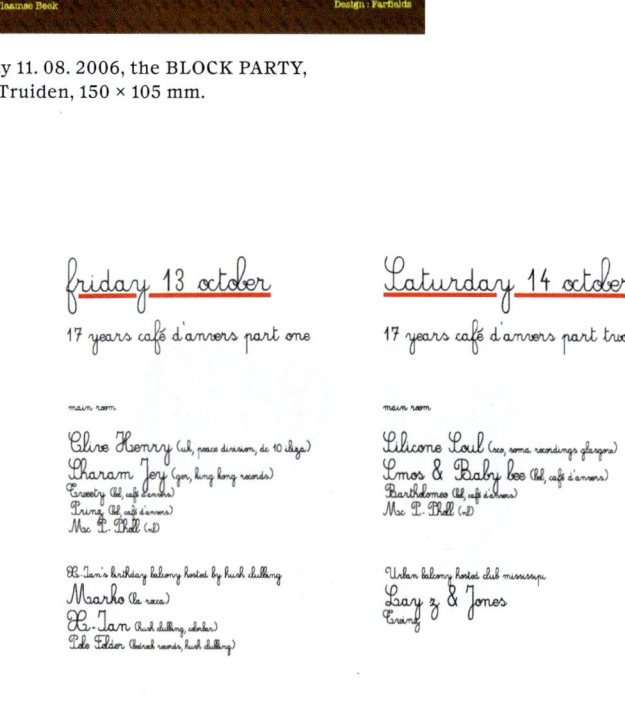

October 2006, *17 years CDA* at Café d'Anvers,
Antwerp, 145 × 105 mm.

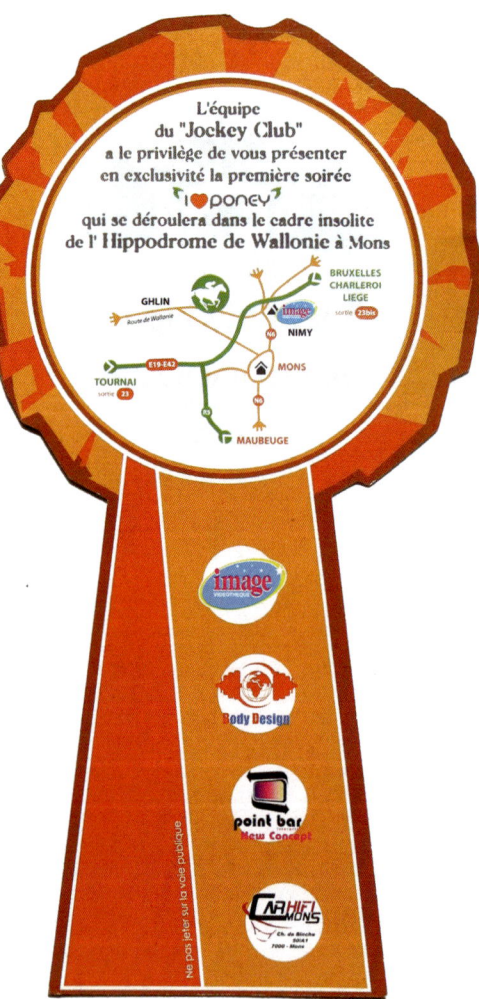

Saturday 25. 11. 2006, *Jockey Club* at l'Hippodrome
de Wallonie, Mons, 200 × 108 mm.

158 2006

April & May 2006, Stereo Sushi, Antwerp, 210 × 148 mm.

October 2006, Stereo Sushi, Antwerp, 210 × 148 mm.

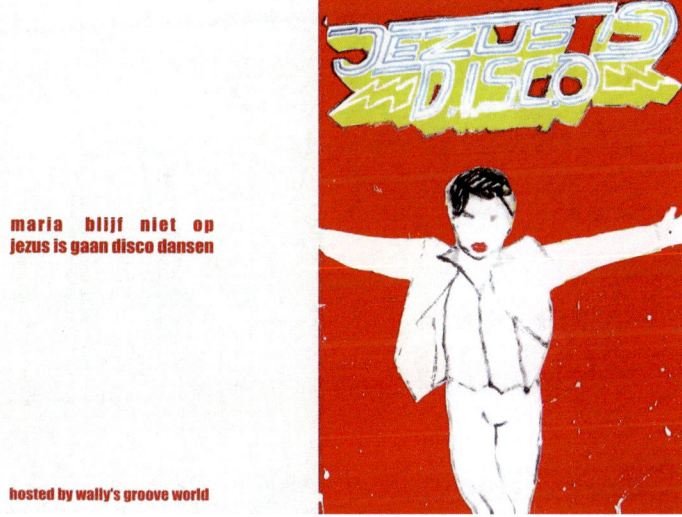

Sunday 24. 12. 2006, *Jezus Is Disco* at Café Capital, Antwerp, 210 × 148 mm.

Sunday 06. 08. 2006, *Xtracity* at Fake Bar, Antwerp, 197 × 37 mm.

Friday 08. 12. 2006, *Push It* at Café d'Anvers, Antwerp, 150 × 105 mm.

April & May 2006, Stereo Sushi,
Antwerp, 210 × 148 mm.

October 2006, Stereo Sushi, Antwerp, 210 × 148 mm.

Sunday 24. 12. 2006, *Jezus Is Disco* at Café Capital,
Antwerp, 210 × 148 mm.

Friday 08. 12. 2006, *Push It*
at Café d'Anvers, Antwerp, 150 × 105 mm.

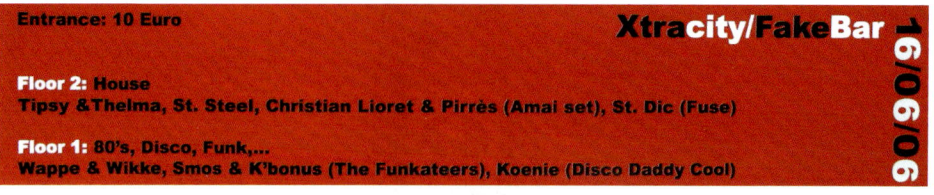

Sunday 06. 08. 2006, *Xtracity*
at Fake Bar, Antwerp, 197 × 37 mm.

January, February, March, April, May, June, October & December 2007, Café d'Anvers, Antwerp, 145 × 105 mm.

June 2007, Café d'Anvers, Antwerp, 150 × 105 mm.

Saturday 12. 05. 2007, Café d'Anvers, Antwerp, 150 × 105 mm.

December 2007, Café d'Anvers, Antwerp, 150 × 105 mm.

October 2007, Café d'Anvers, Antwerp, 150 × 105 mm.

Wednesday 31. 10. 2007, *18 years CDA* at Café d'Anvers, Antwerp, 210 × 148 mm.

Saturday 23. 06. 2007, *Klank!* at Brasserie Le Roy, Charleroi, 120 × 120 mm.

September 2007, Café d'Anvers, Antwerp, 210 × 148 mm.

Saturday 23. 06. 2007, *Klank!* at Brasserie Le Roy, Charleroi, 120 × 120 mm.

Saturday 04. 08. 2007, *The Bassment In Motion* at Jeugdhuis Spiraal, Rijkevorsel, 210 × 148 mm.

Wednesday 16. 05. 2007, *21st Century Club* at Waagnatie, Antwerp, 150 × 150 mm.

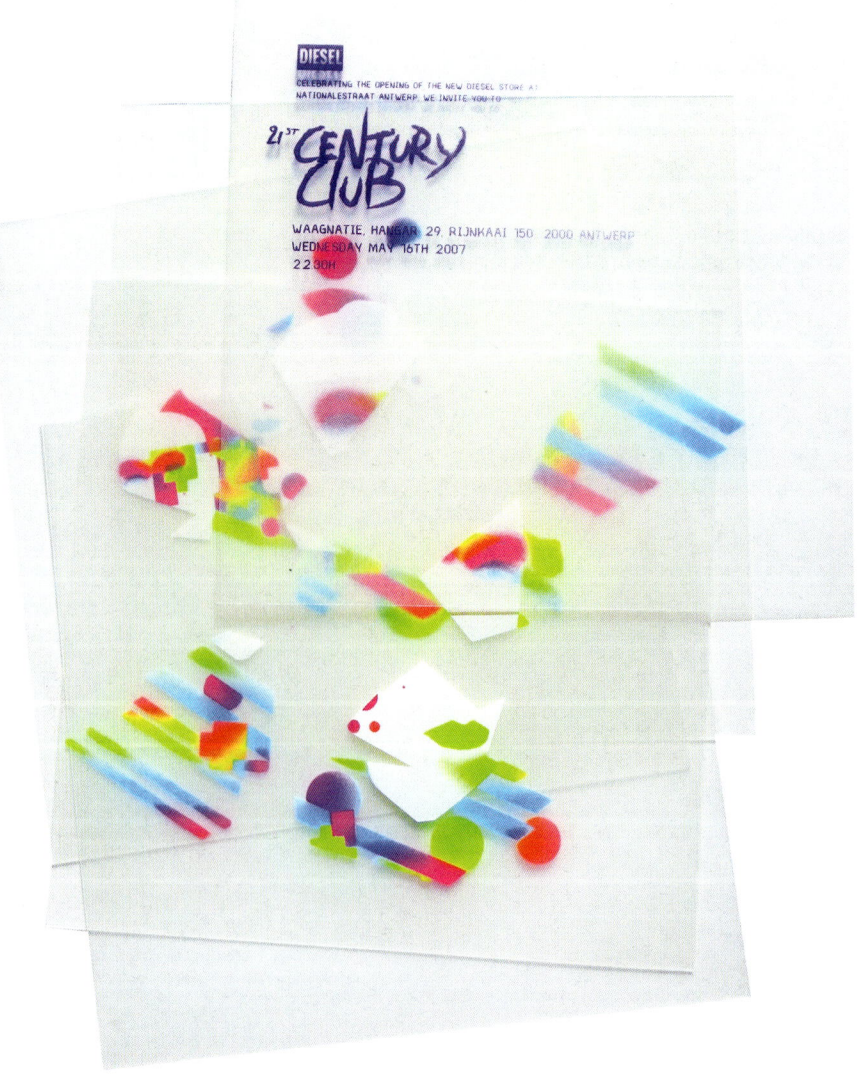

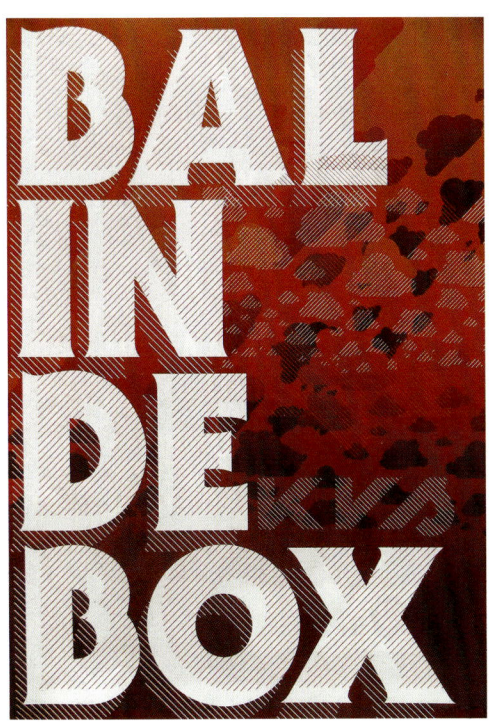

Saturday 07. 04. 2007, *Bal In De Box* at KVS, Brussels, 150 × 105 mm.

Saturday 27. 01. 2007, *PLAY* at Forest Festival, Kwatrecht, 150 × 105 mm.

Friday 22. 06. 2007, *ELECTRIFIED* at Cinécafé, Herentals, 150 × 105 mm.

June 2007, Make-Up, Ghent, 310 × 310 mm.

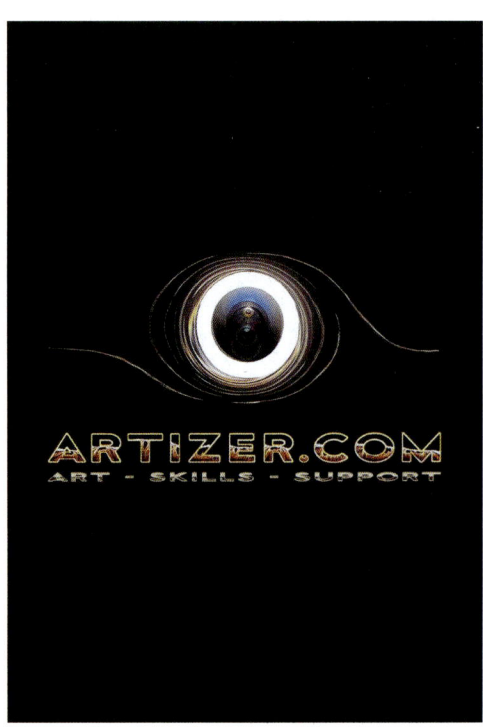

Friday 22. 06. 2007, *ELECTRIFIED* at Cinécafé, Herentals, 150 × 105 mm.

Saturday 27. 01. 2007, *PLAY* at Forest Festival, Kwatrecht, 150 × 105 mm.

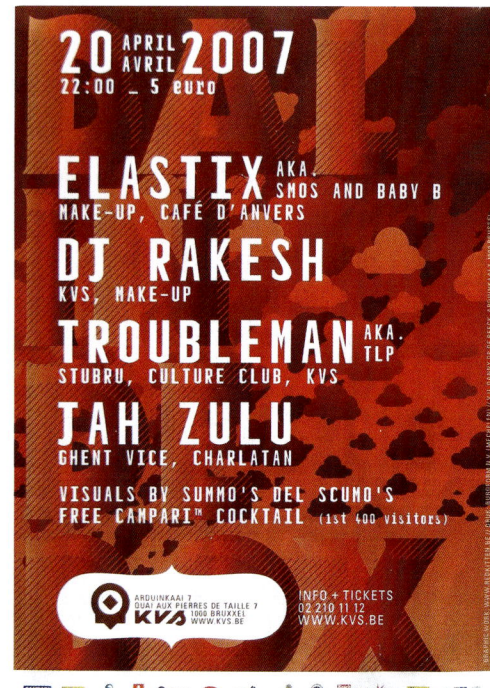

Saturday 07. 04. 2007, *Bal In De Box* at KVS, Brussels, 150 × 105 mm.

June 2007, Make-Up, Ghent, 310 × 310 mm.

July 2007, Tomorrowland,
Boom, 360 × 120 mm.

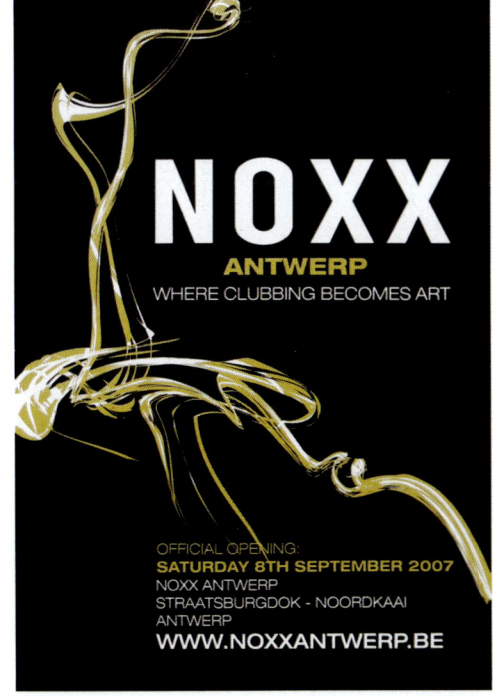

September 2007, Noxx, Antwerp, 210 × 148 mm.

September 2007, *Goodlife*
at Café Capital, Antwerp, 290 × 210 mm.

July 2007, Tomorrowland,
Boom, 360 × 120 mm.

September 2007, *Goodlife*
at Café Capital, Antwerp, 290 × 210 mm.

September 2007, Noxx, Antwerp, 210 × 148 mm.

November 2007, Café Capital,
Antwerp, 148 × 148 mm.

October 2007, Café Capital, Antwerp, 148 × 148 mm.

Saturday 10. 11. 2007, *Paradise*
at Café d'Anvers, Antwerp, 145 × 145 mm.

Saturday 01. 09. 2007,
Laundry Day, Antwerp, 104 × 75 mm.

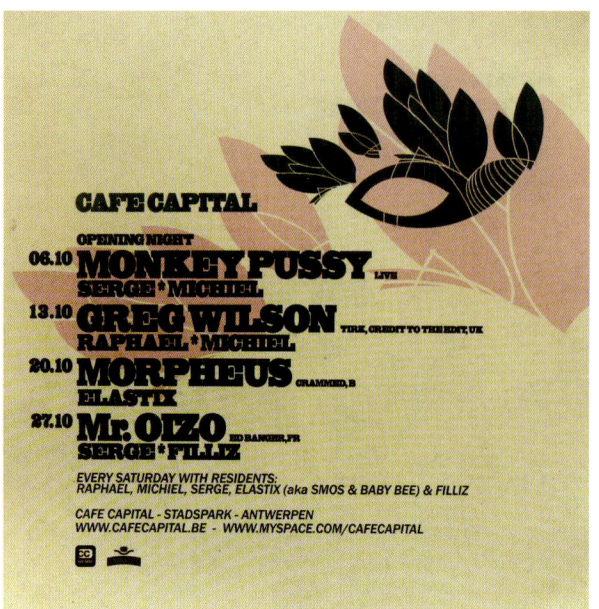

October 2007, Café Capital, Antwerp, 148 × 148 mm.

November 2007, Café Capital, Antwerp, 148 × 148 mm.

Saturday 01. 09. 2007, Laundry Day, Antwerp, 104 × 75 mm.

Saturday 10. 11. 2007, *Paradise* at Café d'Anvers, Antwerp, 145 × 145 mm.

Friday 05. 01. 2007, *The Heavies*
at Café Capital, Antwerp, 104 × 75 mm.

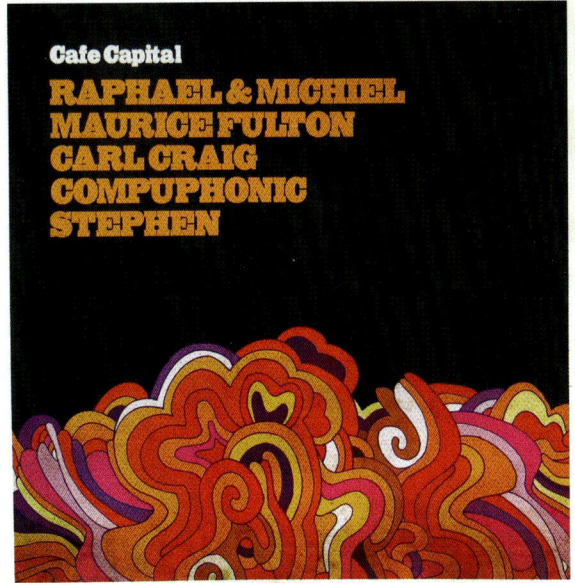

December 2007, Café Capital,
Antwerp, 148 × 148 mm.

Saturday 13. 10. 2007, Soulshine Festival,
Boechout, 208 × 98 mm.

November & December 2007,
Make-Up, Ghent, 150 × 105 mm.

December 2007, Café Capital,
Antwerp, 148 × 148 mm.

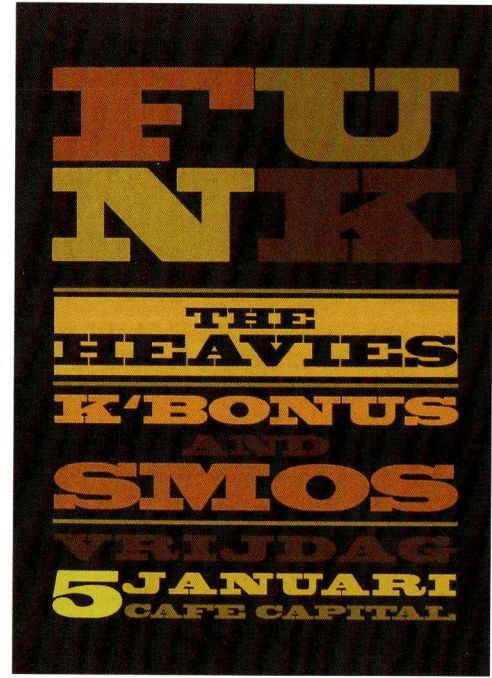

Friday 05. 01. 2007, *The Heavies*
at Café Capital, Antwerp, 104 × 75 mm.

Saturday 13. 10. 2007, Soulshine Festival,
Boechout, 208 × 98 mm.

November & December 2007, Make-Up,
Ghent, 150 × 105 mm.

January 2008, *Play* at Café Capital,
Antwerp, 150 × 105 mm.

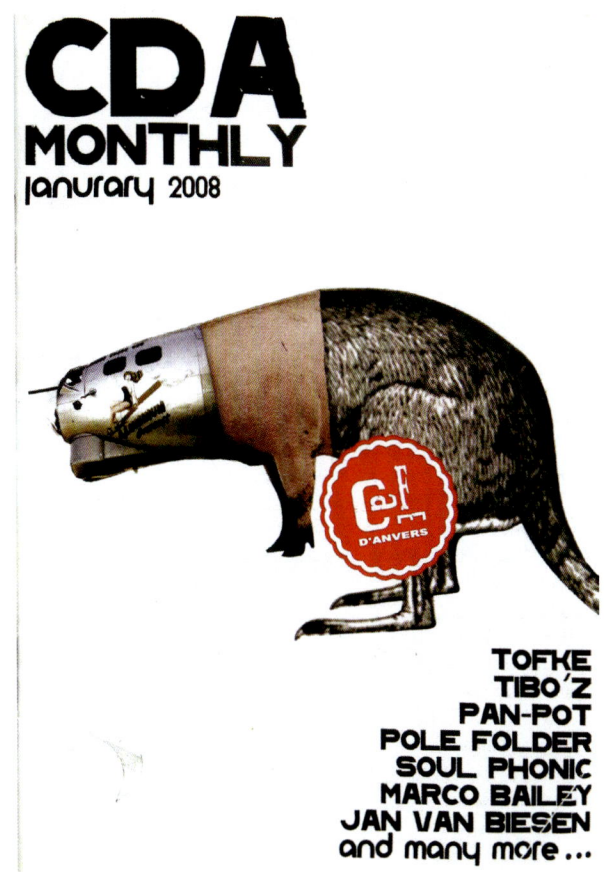

January 2008, Café d'Anvers, Antwerp,
150 × 105 mm.

Wednesday 30. 01. 2008, *Designers Against Aids* at
Café d'Anvers, Antwerp, 150 × 105 mm.

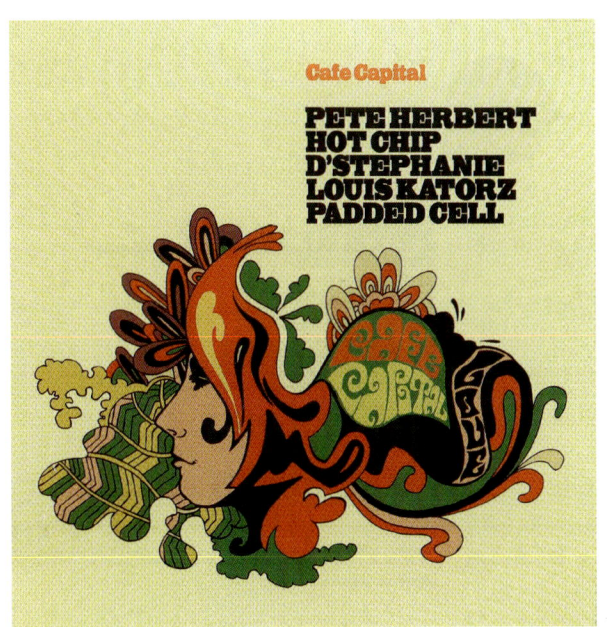

January 2008, Café Capital,
Antwerp, 150 × 150 mm.

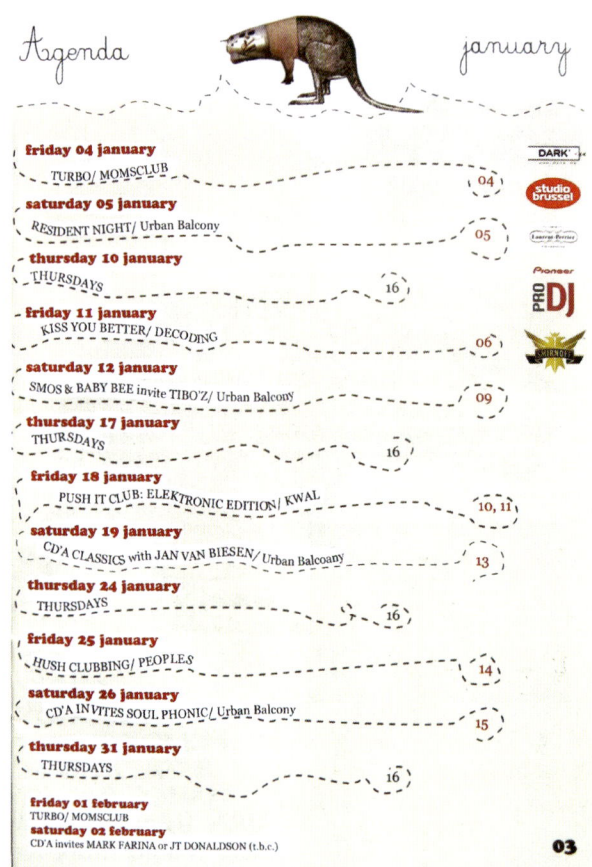

January 2008, Café d'Anvers, Antwerp, 150 × 105 mm.

January 2008, *Play* at Café Capital, Antwerp, 150 × 105 mm.

January 2008, Café Capital, Antwerp, 150 × 150 mm.

Wednesday 30. 01. 2008, *Designers Against Aids* at Café d'Anvers, Antwerp, 150 × 105 mm.

February & March. 2008, Café Capital,
Antwerp, 150 × 150 mm.

February 2008, Café d'Anvers,
Antwerp, 150 × 105 mm.

March 2008, Stereo Sushi,
Antwerp, 98 × 208 mm.

February, March & April 2008, Stereo Sushi,
Antwerp, 150 × 105 mm.

Saturday 03. 05. 2008, Openlucht Fuif,
Brasschaat, 150 × 105 mm.

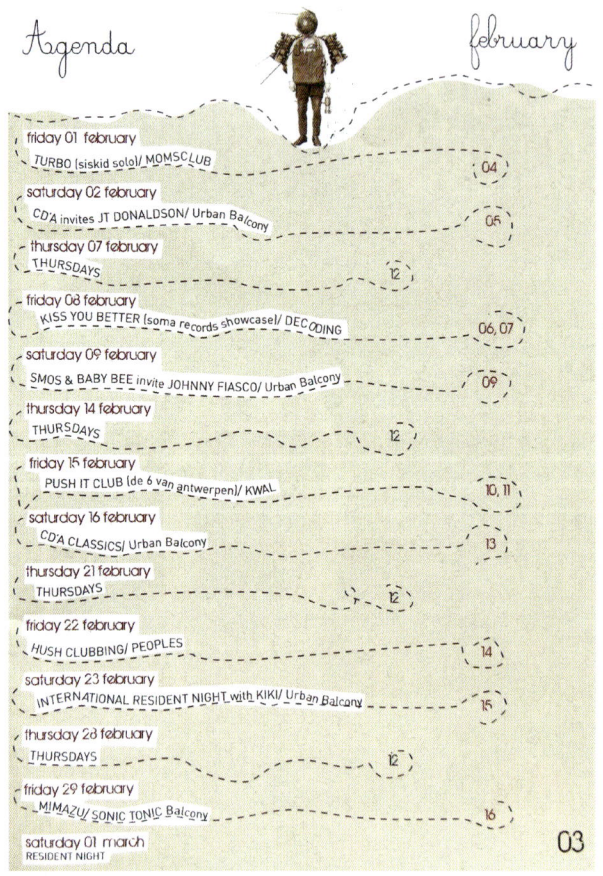

February 2008, Café d'Anvers,
Antwerp, 150 × 105 mm.

February & March. 2008, Café Capital,
Antwerp, 150 × 150 mm.

Saturday 03. 05. 2008, Openlucht Fuif,
Brasschaat, 150 × 105 mm.

February, March & April 2008, Stereo Sushi,
Antwerp, 150 × 105 mm.

March 2008, Stereo Sushi,
Antwerp, 98 × 208 mm.

April 2008, Café d'Anvers, Antwerp, 150 × 105 mm.

March 2008, Café d'Anvers, Antwerp, 150 × 105 mm.

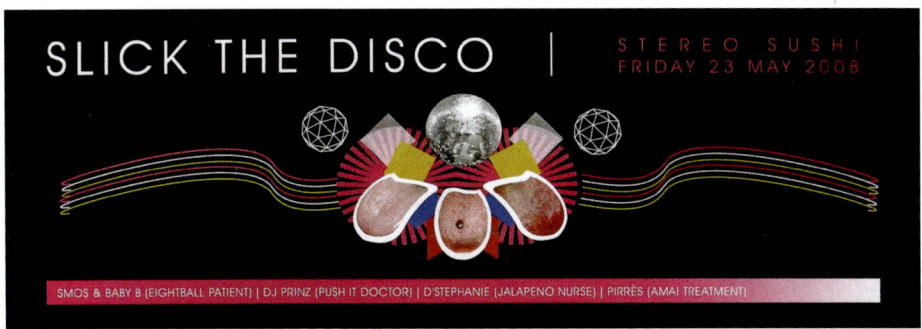

Friday 23. 05. 2008, *Slick The Disco* at Stereo Sushi, Antwerp, 98 × 208 mm.

May & June 2008, Café Capital, Antwerp, 208 × 98 mm.

March 2008, Café d'Anvers, Antwerp, 150 × 105 mm.

April 2008, Café d'Anvers, Antwerp, 150 × 105 mm.

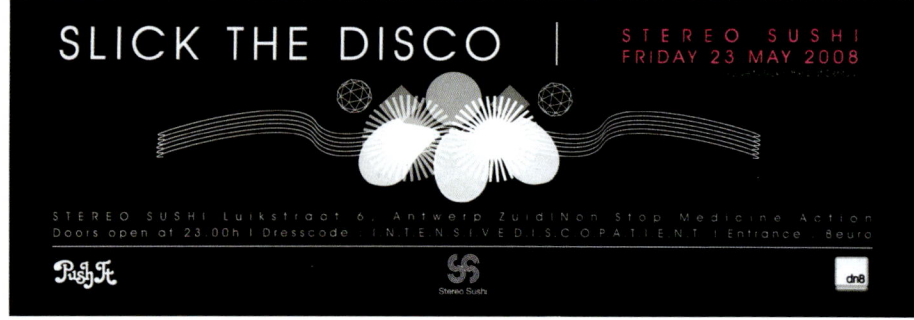

Friday 23. 05. 2008, *Slick The Disco*
at Stereo Sushi, Antwerp, 98 × 208 mm.

May & June 2008, Café Capital,
Antwerp, 208 × 98 mm.

April & May 2008, Café Capital,
Antwerp, 208 × 98 mm.

May 2008, Stereo Sushi,
Antwerp, 150 × 105 mm.

June 2008, Café d'Anvers,
Antwerp, 150 × 105 mm.

April & May 2008, Café Capital, Antwerp, 208 × 98 mm.

May 2008, Stereo Sushi, Antwerp, 150 × 105 mm.

June 2008, Café d'Anvers, Antwerp, 150 × 105 mm.

August & September 2008,
Petrol, Antwerp, 150 × 105 mm.

Saturday 26. 07. 2008, *Parklife*
at Café Capital, Antwerp, 297 × 210 mm.

July & August 2008,
Café d'Anvers, Antwerp, 150 × 105 mm.

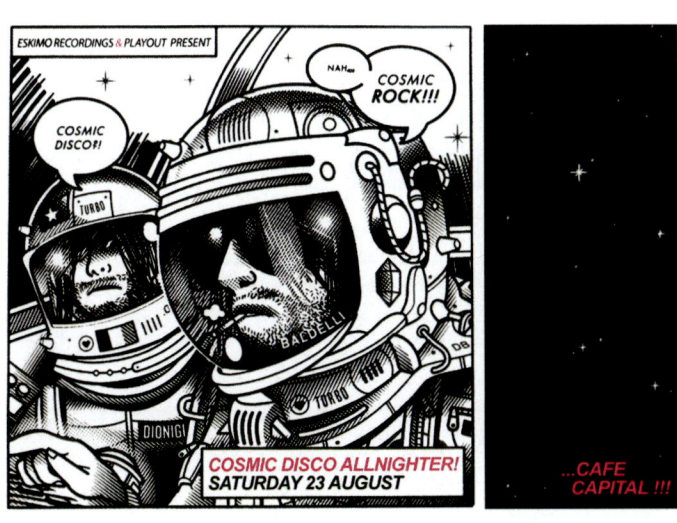

Saturday 23. 08. 2008, *Cosmic Disco Allnighter* at
Café Capital, Antwerp, 150 × 105 mm.

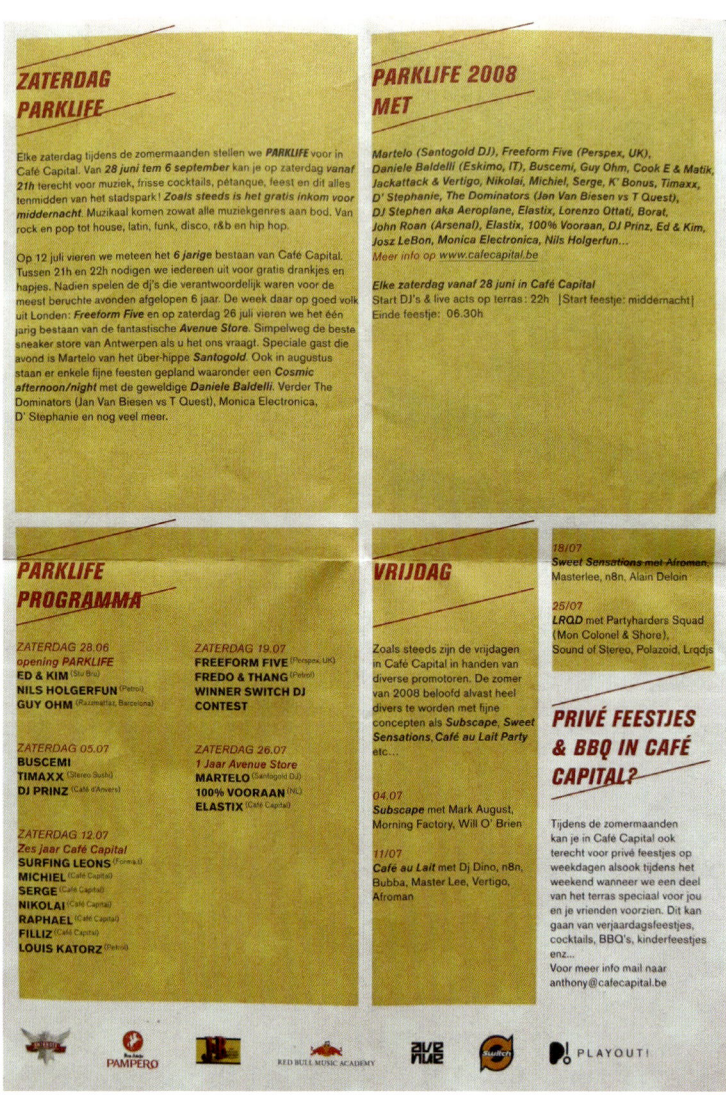

Saturday 26. 07. 2008, *Parklife*
at Café Capital, Antwerp, 297 × 210 mm.

Saturday 23. 08. 2008, *Cosmic Disco Allnighter* at
Café Capital, Antwerp, 150 × 105 mm.

August & September 2008,
Petrol, Antwerp, 150 × 105 mm.

July & August 2008,
Café d'Anvers, Antwerp, 150 × 105 mm.

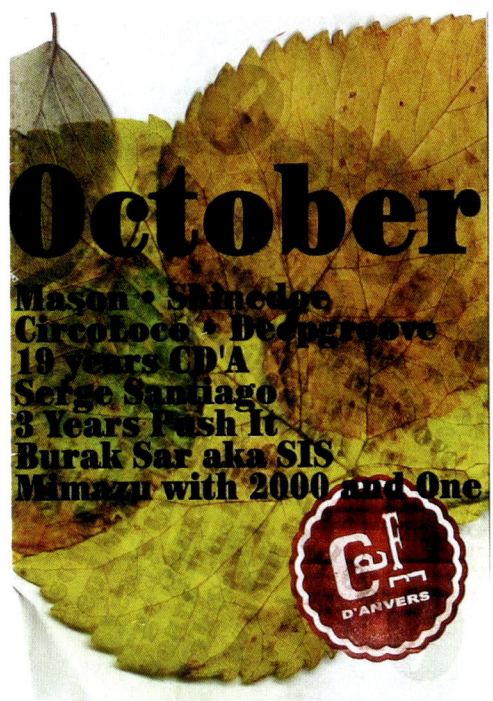

October 2008, Café d'Anvers,
Antwerp, 150 × 105 mm.

November & December 2008,
Café d'Anvers, Antwerp, 150 × 105 mm.

November 2008, *Play*
at Café Capital, Antwerp, 208 × 98 mm.

Saturday 06. 09. 2008,
Laundry Day, Antwerp, 105 × 73 mm.

DECEMBER 2008

Thu 04/12/08 THURSDAYS p.18
Fri 05/12/08 MIMAZU WITH WIGHNOMY BROTHERS p.22
Sat 06/12/08 CD'A INVITES SEBO K p.23
Thu 11/12/08 THURSDAYS p.18
Fri 12/12/08 KISS YOU BETTER WITH TIGER STRIPES p.24
Sat 13/12/08 SMOS AND BABY BEE INVITE
FABRICE LIG (DJ SET) / SOUL DESIGNER (LIVE) p.25
Thu 18/12/08 THURSDAYS p.18
Fri 19/12/08 PUSH IT CLUB DE 6 VAN ANTWERPEN p.26
Sat 20/12/08 CD'A INVITES SPENCER PARKER p.27
Wed 24/12/08 FRESH2DEF XL CHRISTMAS EDITION p.28
Thu 25/12/08 THURSDAYS p.18
Fri 26/12/08 ELECTRONATION WITH POPOF p.29
Sat 27/12/08 INTERNATIONAL RESIDENT NIGHT WITH
SILICONE SOUL p.30
Wed 31/12/08 NYE / 20 YEARS OF HOUSEMUSIC p.32

November & December 2008,
Café d'Anvers, Antwerp, 150 × 105 mm.

October 2008, Café d'Anvers,
Antwerp, 150 × 105 mm.

Yezzz ! 't is weer zover ! Zaterdag 6 september

The fracking coolest fantastic festival of the Galaxy.

11 stages, meer dan 100 Dj's èn live-groepen.

Beats, breaks en fashion
op de kasseien van het Eilandje.
En natuurlijk ... lots of fun. Yiehaaa !

Zet die dag in je agenda in dubbele fluo !
't Is trouwens de eerste zaterdag van het nieuwe
schooljaar, tijd voor een serieuze break.

No shit, no excuses... Be there !

MAY DE WAS BE WITH YOU

Damage : presale 10€, doors 15€ - Tickets & line up, check WWW.LAUNDRYDAY.BE

Saturday 06. 09. 2008,
Laundry Day, Antwerp, 105 × 73 mm.

November 2008, *Play*
at Café Capital, Antwerp, 208 × 98 mm.

July 2008, Tomorrowland, Boom, 120 × 120 mm.

December 2008, *Play* at Café Capital, Antwerp, 150 × 105 mm.

Saturday 06. 12. 2008, *Lollipop* at Opus Dancing Hall, Tournai, 150 × 105 mm.

Friday 19. 12. 2008, *Push It* at Café d'Anvers, Antwerp, 150 × 105 mm.

July 2008, Tomorrowland, Boom, 360 × 120 mm.

Friday 19. 12. 2008, *Push It*
at Café d'Anvers, Antwerp, 150 × 105 mm.

Saturday 06. 12. 2008, *Lollipop*
at Opus Dancing Hall, Tournai, 150 × 105 mm.

December 2008, *Play* at Café Capital,
Antwerp, 150 × 105 mm.

April 2009, *Play* at Café Capital,
Antwerp, 148 × 148 mm.

March *&* April 2009, Café Capital,
Antwerp, 210 × 100 mm.

February 2009, Café d'Anvers,
Antwerp, 145 × 105 mm.

April 2009, Café d'Anvers,
Antwerp, 145 × 105 mm.

March & April 2009, Café Capital,
Antwerp, 210 × 100 mm.

April 2009, *Play* at Café Capital,
Antwerp, 148 × 148 mm.

April 2009, Café d'Anvers,
Antwerp, 145 × 105 mm.

February 2009, Café d'Anvers,
Antwerp, 145 × 105 mm.

July 2009, Tomorrowland, Boom, 360 × 120 mm.

December 2009, Café d'Anvers, Antwerp, 145 × 105 mm.

May & June 2009, Café d'Anvers, Antwerp, 145 × 105 mm.

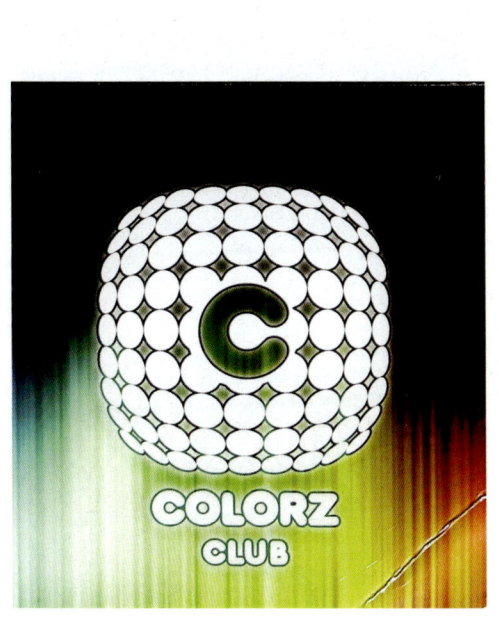

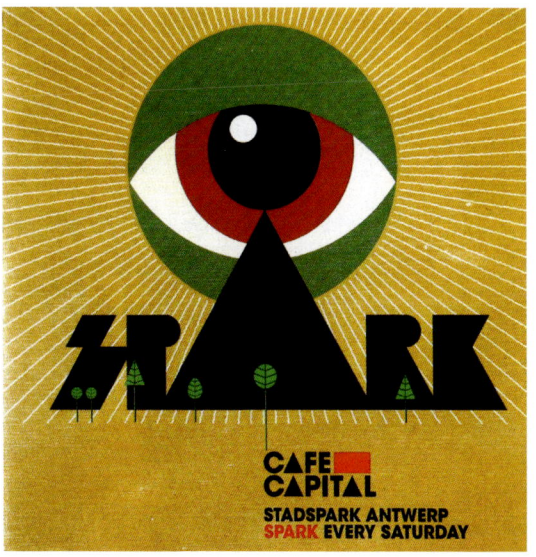

September 2009, *Spark* at Café Capital, Antwerp, 120 × 120 mm.

April 2009, Colorz Club, Mons, 296 × 100 mm.

July 2009, Tomorrowland,
Boom, 360 × 120 mm.

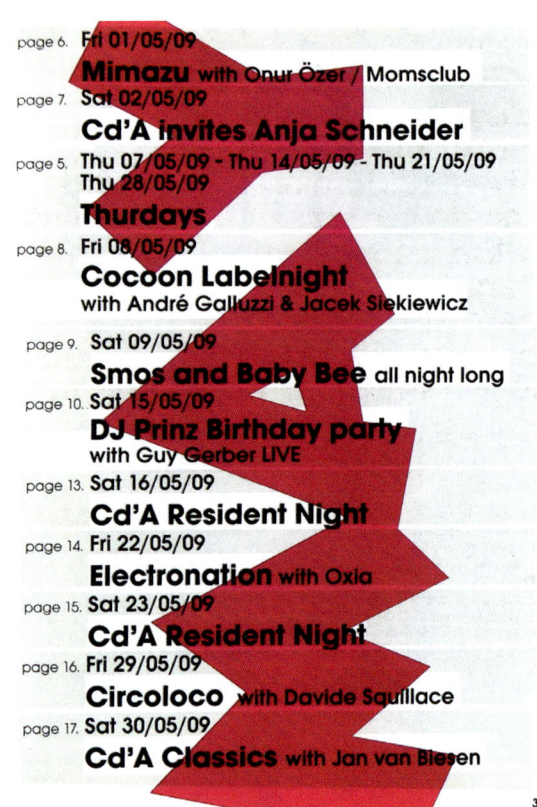

May & June 2009, Café d'Anvers,
Antwerp, 145 × 105 mm.

September 2009, *Spark* at Café Capital,
Antwerp, 120 × 120 mm.

April 2009, Colorz Club, Mons, 296 × 100 mm.

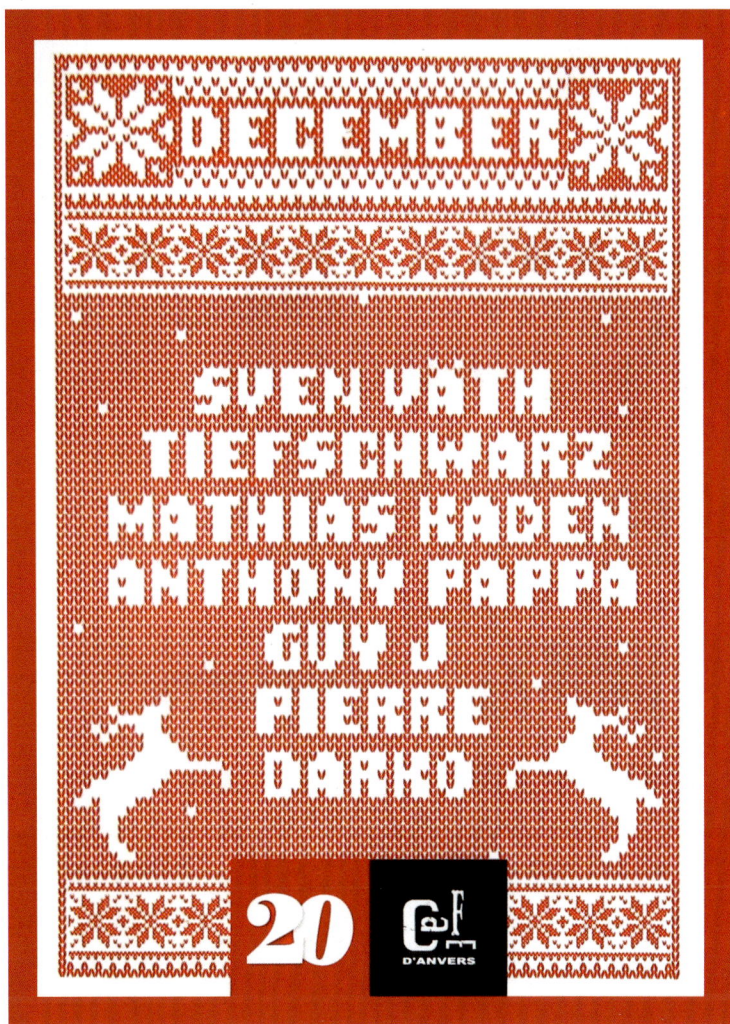

Thursday 31. 12. 2009,
Café d'Anvers, Antwerp, 145 × 105 mm.

September 2009, Café d'Anvers,
Antwerp, 145 × 105 mm.

October. 2009, Café d'Anvers,
Antwerp, 145 × 105 mm.

DECEMBER 2009

THU 03
THURSDAYS
main room
RALF

urban balcony
SEROM & ASFALTE

Free Entrance

FRI 04
MIMAZU PRESENTS STUDIO 10 ALBUMTOUR
main room
MATHIAS KADEN
Gera-Jena / Vakant – Freude Am Tanzen
CLAR & CAMEO
Mimazu Residents

balcony
CLOSED!

More info page 8-9

SAT 05
CD'A INVITES HERMANEZ
main room
HERMANEZ
Miconn Rec. – Café d'Anvers
BARTHOLOMEO
PATRICK SCHMIDT

Club Trace
TM & VISTA

THU 10
THURSDAYS
main room
RALF

urban balcony
SEROM & ASFALTE

Free Entrance

FRI 11
PEOPLES
main room
ANTHONY PAPPA
London / Global Underground – Renaissance
GUY J
Tel Aviv / Bedrock Rec. – Turbo Rec
PHILIP MICHAEL ANDERSSON
Faith Music – La Rocca

Lucas Pereri's Bday balcony
LUCAS PERERI
Faith Music
SHARP
Faith Music
DAVE PHENTON
Magic Hall
FELIS
Magic Hall - Discovery
MINIMAL KILLERS
Ambiosphere Rec.
DOUM
Prestige Concept

More info page 10-11

SAT 12
SMOS AND BABY BEE ALL NIGHT LONG
main room
SMOS & BABY BEE
Café d'Anvers

Club Trace
MAD-D & A-STARZ

THU 17
THURSDAYS
main room
RALF

urban balcony
SEROM & ASFALTE

Free Entrance

Thursday 31. 12. 2009,
Café d'Anvers, Antwerp, 145 × 105 mm.

October. 2009, Café d'Anvers,
Antwerp, 145 × 105 mm.

September 2009, Café d'Anvers,
Antwerp, 145 × 105 mm.

DJ INDEX

A

A Mountain Of One
A-Starz
A-Tek
Aardvarck
Ab
Abe Duque
Above & Beyond
Ac/DJ
Acid Kirk's
 Psychonauts
Adam Beyer
Adam F
Adam Freeland
Aeroplane aka
 DJ Stephen
Afrojack
Afroman aka Dimitri
Aft.erhours
Agent K1x
Agoria
Aim
Airwave
Akufen
Alain Deloin
Alain Faber
Alan Russel
Aldo
Alec
Alex
Alex Gaudino
Alex Gopher
Alex Klimow
Alex Paterson
Alex Reece
Alex Smoke
Alex Under
Alexander Kowalski
Alexander Robotnick
Alexi Delano
Alexia
Alexkid
Alfonso
Alfredo
Alien Ness
Alpha2
Alter Ego
Alton Miller
Amanda Bergdorf
Amir Javasoul

Anat Ben David
Andre Pinguin
Andreas Lang
Andreas Pils
Andrew Weatherall
André
André 'Eurosong'
 Vermeulen
André De Vitta
André Galluzi
Andy C
Andy Caldwell
Andy Jarrod
Andy Moor
Angel Moraes
Angelo
Anja Schneider
Anthony
Anthony Pappa
Anthony Rother
Anton Price
Ao-Tec
Aorta 'n Kash
Aphex Twin
Aphrodite
Aqua Bassino
Arcana
Archimad
Ares
Argy
Aril Brikha
Arkanoid
Armand Van Helden
Armandi
Armani
Armatt
Armin Van Buuren
Arnout
Arsenal
Art-B
Asad Rizvi
Asfalte
Astral Projection
Astrix
Ata
Atjazz
Attaboy
Aubrey
Audiofly
Aurore
Autechre

Automan
Aventis
Axel Daeseleire
Axell
Axl.
Axwell
Azzido Da Bass
Âme

B

B-Art
B.Watt
B12
Basement Jaxx
Bad Company
Baggio
Bailey
Barbara
Barbara Tucker
Barem
Barry Fore
Bart
Bart M.
Bart Maes
Bartholomeo
Basement
 Sound Crew
Basic
Bassculture
Bassment
Bastian
Basto!
Battles
Baz
Beanfield
 & Syrup
Beat Ben
Beatblenderz
Beatnix
Beholder
 & Balistic
Ben & Nolle
Ben Biets
Ben Dover's
 Booty Duty
Ben Sims
Ben Watt
Ben Wilcox
Benaldo

& Edmundo
Benjamin
Benjamin Diamond
Benn
Benny Rodrigues
Berkson & What
Bern
Bernard & Bernard
Bernard Dobbeleer
Bernard Gavilan
Bert
Bert Bril
Bertrand Jacques
Biens
Big Bert
Big Boy Caprice
Big Train
Bill Riley
Billy Nasty
Binci V
Binum
Bj-Jules
Bjørn Db
Black & Dekker
Black Frank
Black Strobe
Blackjack
Blake Baxter
Blake Jarrell
Bloc Party
Bo & Khilla
Bob & Rod
Bob Sinclar
Bobby Speed
Bodyrox
Bola
Bolle
Bomb O Matic
Bomboola Prod
Bongo Allen
Boomba Maka 'O
Borat
Boris Romanov
  & Fish
Born To
  Jazz Movement
Boulou
Brandy
Brassmonkey
Brayn Zentz
Brazzmonkey
Brekbit
Brennan Heart
Brett Johnson
Brian G &
  Mc Fearless
Brian V
Briskey
British Murder Boys
Broertjes Verdonck
Brooks
Brown Moshunz
Bryan
Bryan Gee
Bryan Zentz
Bryand
Bubba
Buckfunk 3000
Bud Bumper
Bugsy n Jensen
Bun-Zero
Bunker Label
Burak Sar Aka Sis
Burger/Voigt
Buscemi

C

Cajmere
aka Green Velvet
Calyx
Candyman D
Capetown
Captain Comatose
Cari Lekebusch
Carl Cox
Carl Craig
Carl Craig's
Paperclip People
Carlijn
Carlos
Cartel De Lux
ft. Juanito
  Infinito & Steff
Cash Money
Casper
Cedd
Cedric De Pauw
Celtric
Cesar De Molero
Chaib
Chal-Zee
Chantal
Chari Vari
Charles
Charles Schillings
Charles Siegling
Charles Webster
Chateau Flight
Chateau Flight
  ft. I-Cube
Chen
Chess
Chicago Zone
Chicken Lips
Chicks On Speed
Chloé
Chris
Chris Gainer
Chris Liebing
Chris Lioret
Chris Woodward
Chrisstcrash
Christian Smith
Christian Vogel

Chuckie
Chunk
Château Lamotte
Ciccio
Cimaï
Cinérex
Circoloco
CJ Bolland
Clar & Cameo
Claude Von Stroke
Claude Young
Clauz
Climaxx
Clive Henry
Clive Morgan
Clémentine
Cobblestone Jazz
Common
Compuphonic
Cook E & Matik
Coone
Copyright
Corrid'Or
Cosmic
Cosmic & Sake
Cosy Mozzy
Count Vasily
Cp
Craig Mcgivern
Craig Richards
Crash Res
Crisp
Cristian Vogel
Cubanate
Cute
Cypress Hill
Cyril K
Cé Cé M.
Cécém

D

dBridge & Sp:Mc
D Convict
D'Ache
D'Ache & D'Elle
D'Julz
D'Stephanie
D'Stephanie
  & Melissa
D-Block &
  S-Te-Fan
D-Nice
D-Tale
D-Virus
D.J. Johnson
D.J. Quinten
Da Book
Da House Corps
Dacosta
Dada Life
Daddy Cool

Dago
Damian Lazarus
Dan Ghenacia
Dana
Daniel Abrandis
Daniel Bovie
  & Roy Rox
Daniele Baldelli
Daniele Poli
Danny Breaks
Danny C
Danny Howells
Danny Krivit
Danny V.
Danton Eeprom
Daphne
Daquan
Darko
Darren Emerson
Darren Price
Darren Roach
Das Pop
Dash
Dava
Dave & Sam
Dave Angel
Dave Clarke
Dave Ellesmere
Dave Hill
Dave Lambert
Dave Phenton
Dave Tarrida
David
David Alvarado
David Dummy
David Duriez
David Guetta
David Holmes
David Hoover
David Morales
Davide Squillace
Davidov
Davidov Vs Mystique
Daviz
Davy D.
Davyd
Daz Quayle
Daz Sound
De Hop Allstars
Deep Dish
Deepack
Deepgroove
Deetron
Deg
Dego
Demon
Den Hetrix
Denis
Dennis Ferrer
Derrick Carter
Derrick May
Desk & Uinkxx
Detroit Grand Pubahs
Deviera
Dexter
Dexter Malkom
Di'Jital
Diablo
Dice
Didier D. Olivier
Didski & Zohm
Diephuis DJ'S
Diepvries
Diesel
Dijf Sanders
Dimaro
Dimitri
Dimitri 'Boenox'
  Brusselmans
Dimitri From Paris
Dimitri Vegas
  & Like Mike
Dimiz
Dirk
Dirk Diggler
Dirty Jos Soundsystem
Dirty South
Disco Devil
Disco Soup
Discobar Galaxie
Dixon
DJ 4T4
DJ Aki
DJ Assault
DJ B
DJ Babybang
DJ Ball
DJ Balthazar
DJ Buzz
DJ Chloe
DJ Clementine
DJ Cosmo
DJ Cyrix
DJ Dan
DJ Deep
DJ Dino
DJ Disciple
DJ Diz
DJ Dizel
DJ Dk
DJ Elof
DJ Eric B
DJ Feadz
DJ Fetisch
DJ Fire
DJ Fra
DJ Frederico
DJ Funk
DJ G-Pop
DJ Gee
DJ Ghost
DJ Godfather
DJ Goodgroove
DJ Gregory
DJ Handic
DJ Harvey
DJ Heather
DJ Hell
DJ Hikke
DJ Jean
DJ Juhlo
DJ Jules Deelder
DJ K
DJ Kevin
DJ Kool
DJ Koze
DJ Krush
DJ Licious
DJ Low
DJ Lucien Foort
DJ Luck-E
DJ Marko
DJ Marky
DJ Mehdi
DJ Mellow & Red Ant
DJ Meniac
DJ Mes
DJ Miss Ann
DJ Morpheus
DJ Moss
DJ Mozz
DJ Naughty
DJ Nicolas
DJ Olivier
DJ Paniekzaaier
DJ Pierre
DJ Premier
  & Big Shug
DJ Prinz
DJ Psar
DJ Q
DJ Quint
DJ Rakesh
DJ Ralf
DJ Rap
DJ Remy & Roland
  Klinkenberg
DJ Rudy
DJ Rush
DJ Sash!
DJ Sneak
DJ Soi
DJ Spinna
DJ Spooky
DJ T.
DJ Team Radio Urgent
DJ Thomas Morr
DJ Tourist
DJ Tuttle
DJ Uinkxxs
DJ Valium
DJ Vertesse
DJ Ward
DJ Yellow
DJ Zinc
DJ Smoove
DJ'S Are Not Rockstars
  (Princess Superstar +
  Alexander Technique)

DJames
DJeff
DJerom
DJorivo
DJorvin Clain
DJr
DJuma Soundsystem
DMX Krew
Dnb Goony
Dobe 'n' Daze
Doc Martin
Doc Scott
Doc Vinyl
Doctor Disco
Dom & Roland
Domenic Cappello
Dominico
Dominik Eulberg
Don Cabron
Don Collins
Don Juan
   De Naranja
Don Santos
Donkey Rollers
Donn Johnson
Dorian
Dors
Double Axl
Double Jan
Doum
Dpace DJz
Dr Eguobhum
Dr Feelgood
Dr. Desk
Dr. Disco
Dr. Disco
   & King Kitsch
Dr. Lektroluv
Dr. Motte
Dr. Rockit
Dre
Drezz
Drumatizers M.N.
   Blue & Biaz
Dubfire
Dubtales

E

E-Fect & O-Tec
E-Max
E-Phonk
E-Z Rollers
E.Wout
Eavesdropper
Eboman
Echoboy
Ectomorph
Ed & Kim
Ed Dmx
Ed Rush
Ed Rush & Mc Justyce

Ed Rush & Optical
Eddie Adams
Eddy De Clercq
Edeez
Eef
Eerik
El Carlitto
El Kaynor
El Livino
El-Chicano
El-P
Elastix Aka Smos
   & Baby Bee
Electric Indigo
Elemitor
Elias
Elka
Ellen Allien
Emjay
End-Jy
Enzo
Ephedrix
Eric 'Powa' B
Eric Barkman
Eric Borgo
Eric Depage
Eric Nouhan
Eric Rug
Eric Sneo
Erick E
Erik Rug
Erol Alkan
Estim
Etienne De Crecy
Eva
Eva Calzas
Evil Activities
Eye One
Eyeone
Ez Rollers

F

F.E.X.
Fabrice Lig
Factor
Family Affairz
Fanklub DJs
Far West Crew
Fastgraph
Fat
Fauna Flash
Fausto
Faze Action
Fc Kahuna
Felis
Felix Da Housecat
Felix Fuchs
Ferry Corsten
Fila Brazilia
Filip Cortez &
   Juanito Infinto

Filip Dp
Filliz
Filo & Peri
Filterheadz
Filur
Firaga
Flo
Florian Keller
Flowerchild
   And Robob
Flying Dewaele
   Brothers
Foxy Lady
   & Mc Elvee
Franco Cangelli
Frank
Frank & Alex
Frank & Ives
Frank Biazzi
Frank Lorber
Frank Martiniq
Frank Struyf
Frank Zolex
Frankie Knuckles
Franky D
Franky Jones
François Kevorkian
Freaks (Luke Solomon
   & Justin Harris)
Freakz On Deckz
Fred
Fred Hush
Fred Nasen
Fred Nova
Freddy
Freddy Fresh
Frederic
Frederic Galliano
Frederik
FreDJe
Fredo & Thang
Free Vibes
Freeform
Freeform Five
Freestyle Crew
Fresh &
   Mc Stamina
From Disco 2 Disco
Frontliner
Frozen People DJ'S
Frères Deluxe
Fucking
   Dewaele
   Brothers
Fudge
Fun-Q
Funcky Frenic
Funghi
Funk D'Void
Funkstörung
Funky Chocolate
Fussy
Future Forces Inc.

G

G-Flame
G-Force
G. Sportelli
Ganja Kru
Garage Sauvage
Gareth Emery
Gayle San
Gdluxx
Geert
Geht'S Noch
Gemini
Gene Farris
General Midi
Geo
Geoff
Geoffrey
Geoffroid
Geoffroy Aka Mugwump
George Thomsom
George'S
Geosismix
Gerome Sportelli
Gerrit Kerremans
Gert
Gideon Jackson
Gilb'R
Gilbert
Gino
Giuseppe Ottaviani
Glenn
Glimmer Twins
Gms
Goldie
Goldie & Sp:Mc
Gosseries
Grammy
Gravity Wheel
Grazz
Grazzhoppa
Green Velvet
Greenshen
   Soundsystem
Greg Gauthier
Greg Wilson
Gregor Tresher
Groove Addicts
Groove Armada
Groove Cartel
Groove Merchant
Grooverider
Ground Control
Gstaav Pievo & Koen
Guaperas
Gucci Soundsystem
Gui Borrato
Guido Schneider
Guidos
Gus
Guy
Guy Gerber
Guy J
Guy Ohm
   & Funk Frenic
Guy'Do
Guy-Ohm

H

H-Foundation
H.O.S.H
Hank
Hans Oulfer
Hardstyle
Harrison Crump
Havoc & Karbonkid
Headhunterz
Headhunterz &
   Wildstylez
Headman
Headphone
Heavy J
Henk Salon
Henk Vandepapeliere
Henrik Schwarz
Herbert
Hermanez
Hermanos Inglesos
Hernan Cattaneo
Herr Seele
Herrmann & Kleine
Hey Mickey
High Contrast
High Grade Sound
Hmd
Holy Ghost!
Honey Dijon
Hoover
Hot Chip
Housemeister
Hs
Huggy
Huggy Hanton
Hyper
Hügzzz

I

I-F
I:Cube
Ian
Ian O'Brian
Ian Pooley
Ida Engberg
IDJut Boys
Igor
Igwaar
In Sync
Infected Mushroom
Infinito
Irfane
Iris
Irish
Isabel
Isabel & Filliz
Isabel & Tweety
Isabelle
Italoboyz
Ithai
Ivan Smagghe
Ivo

J

J Majik
Jacek Sienkiewicz
Jack
Jack De Marseille
Jaqcues De Marseille
   & Filliz
Jackattack
   & Vertigo
Jacknife Lee
Jacob's Optical
   Stairway
Jacques Renault
Jah Zulu
James
James Holden
James Lavelle
James Pants
James Ruskin
James Zabiela
Jamie Anderson
Jamie Lidell
Jan Eric Kaiser
Jan Van Biesen
Jan Van Biesen
   Vs T-Quest
Jasper Dahlbäck
Jaxx & Jimson
Jay Spinello
Jazz J
Jazzanova
Jb
Jd Twitch
Jean & Paul &
   Alain & Delon
Jean Francois
Jeancedric
Jedi Knights
Jeevee
Jef K
Jeff
Jeff Mills
Jennifer
Jennifer Cardini
Jens H
Jens Holmes
Jens Holmes
   Supported By Bart
   Marisse & Danny
   Van Hoecke
Jensen
Jero Xl

Jerome
Jerome Pacman
Jerome Sydenham
Jes
Jesper
Jesper Dahlbäck
Jesse Rose
Jex N Christian Thomaz
Jezman
Jim
Jimmy Sommerville
Jimpster
Jip Deluxe
Jo
Joachim
Joachim Heldt
Joakim
Jochem
Joe Claussell
Joeri
Joey Beltram
Joey Negro
Johan
Johannes Heil
John 00 Flemming
John Acquaviva
John B
John Cutler
John Dahlbäck
John Digweed
John Helder
John Oo Flemming
John Roan
John Rundell
John Thomas
Johnny Fiasco
Johnny Gold
Johnson
Jolie & A. Lune
Jon Cutler
Jon DaSilva
Jon O'Bir
Jonas Bering
Jonasty
Jones
Jonéné
Joost De Lijser
Joost Van Bellen
Jordy
Jori Hulkkonen
Joris
Joris Voorn
Jos
Jos & Olivier
Jos And Olivier
Josh
Josh & Wesz
Josh Lasden
Josh Michael
Josh Wink
Joss
Josz

Josz & Filliz
Josz LeBon
Josz LeBon & Louis Katorz
Jovonn
Jrd
Jt Donaldson
Juan
Juan Atkins
Juanito Infinito
Juanito Infinito & Felippe Cortez
Juice Blenders
Jul Berbas Aka Nondejul
Jules-X
Junior Jack
Junior Jack & Kid Crème
Jurgen
Jurr
Just Mat
Justin Berkovi
Justin Harris
Justus Kohncke

K

K'Bonus
K-Rim
K-Sys
Kabale Und Liebe
Kaine
Kairon
Kalky
Kandy
Kaos Aka Splay
Karlito
Karma
Karotte
Kash
Kaskade
Kastor & Dice
Kay
Kc The Funkaholic
Keb Darge
Kelley Polar
Ken Ishii
Ken N
Kenneth
Kenneth Cop
Kenny
Kenny Carpenter
Kenny Dope
Kenny Hawkes
Kenny Hawkes & Filliz
Kenny Hawkes & Isabel
Kenny Larkin
Kenshi
Kenson Valdes

Kerri Chandler
Kerstin Eden
Kevin Saunderson
Kevin Yost
Kid Coco
Kiki
Kiki From Silversurfer
Killa Tactics
Kim Peers
Kindred Spirits M.N. Kc The Funkaholic & Mr Wix
King Andre
King Britt
King David
King Size & Gus
Kirk Degiorgio
Knu Red
Koen Janssens
Koen Kampioen
Koenie
Koenie Vs Nikolai
Kojak
Kolombo
Komputerist
Konflict Renegade
Kosheen
Kostas Maskalides
Kozz
Kr!Z
Kraak & Smaak
Kranky
Kreidler
Kretek
Krikor
Kris
Kris & Chris
Kristof P.
Krs
Kruder & Dorfmeister
Krust & Dynamite
Kurd Maverick
Kurt Van Eeghem
Kutmastershok
Kwak
Kwal
Ky
Kyle
Kyulo

L

L-Fêtes
L. Warin
L.Luke
La Gazz
La Issa
Lachka
Lacroix
Lady
Lady Aïda

Lady Jane
Lady Vortex
Lai Yin
Lai-Yin
Laidback Luke
Lani
Larry Mc Cormick
Laston & Geo
Laurent B
Laurent Garnier
Laurent Garnier
   & Scan X
Laurent H
Laurent Top
Laurent Warin
Lawnchair Generals
Lawrens
Lay Z & Jones
Layo & Bushwacka!
Le Chef Tournel
Le Freak
Le Vincent
Lecha
Lee Ching
Lee Holman
Lee Van Dowski
Lefreak
Lefto
Leno
Leo Young
Leon
Leon Bolier
  & Sied Van Riel
Leopard
Lepoard
Les Craven
Les Craven & Filliz
Les Gammas
Les Hommes
Les Petits Pilous
Les Rythmes
  Digitales
Lester Lewitt
Lethal Mg
Level Jay
Lexy & K-Paul
Liaisons D
Liam Shachar
Lickin' Shot
Lindstrom &
  Prins Thomas
Liquid X
Lisa Shaw
Little Louie Vega
Live Sakso & Pacha
Livio & Roby
Llorca
Loco Dice
Loes Lee
London Elektricity
Loop Generation
Lopazz
Loren

Lorenzo
Lorenzo Ottati
Lorin
Losmose
Losoul
Loud-E
Louis
Louis Ferrier
Louis Katorz
Louis.K
Louise Carver
Louke
Loulou Players
Loutka
Lowdown
Lowlands DJ'S
LrqDJs
Lt. Sprüdel
Ltj Bukem
Ltj Bukem & Mc
  Conrad
Luc
Luc Janssen
Luca
Lucas Perreri
Luciano
Lucious
Luck E
Luck E & Mad-D
Ludovic
Luis
Lukas Mooks
Luke Chable
Luke Howard
Luke Slater
Luke Solomon
Luke Vibert
Luna
Lunascape
Lupa
Lyot
Lysergic

M

M.A.N.D.Y.
M.C. Kinky
M8N & Mad-D
Maalik
Macotte
Mad D
Mad Mats
Mad-D & A-Starz
Madman
Magda
Magnus
Maharajazz
Major Tom
Makasi
Maks
Maldo
Mambo Chillum

Mandrak
Mano
Manu
Manual
Manue
Manuel Le Saux
Many Kenton
Many Kentonn
Mar Y Sol
Mara Carlyle
Marc Houle
Marc One & Virus
  Syndicate
Marc Romboy
Marcel Vanthilt
Marcello
Marcello It
Marco
Marco Bailey
Marco Carola
Marco Passarani
Marco Remus
Marco Zaffarano
Marcos
Marcus Intalex
Marino Berardi
Mario Leblanc
Marius
Marius & Samani
Mark August
Mark Broom
Mark C
Mark Farina
Mark Kirby
Mark Knight
Mark Romboy
Mark With A K
Markus Fix
Markus Nikolai
Markus Schulz
Marky
Marnix B.
Martelo
Martin Eyerer
Martin Solveig
Marysol
Mas. Cue
Maskesmachine
Mason
Massimo Dacosta
Massimo Girardi
Massiv Vs The Rebel
Master Lee
Masterz
Mate & Tlp
Mateo & Matos
Mateo And Matos
Mathew Jonson
Mathias Kaden
Mathieu
Matrix
Matt Cantor Of The
  Freestylers

DJ INDEX

Matthew Hawtin
Maurice Fulton
Mauricio Aviles
Maurizio
Mauro
Maurow
Max 404
Max Enforcer
  & Balstic
Max Sedgley
Max Walder
Maxim
Maxim Lany
Maxim Lany &
  Carlitto
Maxime Dangles
Mayaku
Mct
Melvin Lardenoye
Memazz Quintett
Menno De Jong
Menno De Jong
  Vs Estuera
Merdan Taplak
Metrobox
Mi-K
Mic A Nik
Mic Brainstorm
Micanic
Michael Mayer
Michael Reinboth
Michel De Hey
Michel Traxx
Michiel
Mickey
Mickey Finn
Miguel
Miguel Graça
Miguel Migs
Miikha Kuisma
Mikanik
Mike
Mike D.
Mike Grant
Mike L
Mike Thompson
Mikis
Millennium Kru
Millennium Kru
  & Mc Dapper
Mimazu
Mimazu With 2000
  And One
Minidell
Minimal Killers
Miquel Santos
Misc.
Mish Mash
  Soundsystem
Miss Chrisalyde
Miss Clementine
Miss DJax
Miss Elorak-Vanno

Miss Kittin
Miss Monica
Miss Nine
Miss Yeti
Missgwen
Missy Sandra
Mister Bolan
Mixie Mansion
Mo & Benoelie
Mo & Grazz
Mo And Benoelie
Moiano
Monica
Monica Electronica
Monika Kruse
Monkey Pussy
Monolake
Monte La Rue
Moodlex
Moody
Moodymann
Moon
Moose &
  Liol Himself
Morgan Geist
Morning Factory
Morse Inspectors
Mr Binji
Mr Coconut
Mr Jingles
Mr Jon Dasilva
Mr Sam
Mr V
Mr. Binj
Mr. C
Mr. Cheebahawkes
Mr. Crochet
Mr. G-Rald
Mr. Grammy
Mr. Oizo
Mr. Scruff
Mrc & David H
Msc
Mu
Multics
Munk
Murdock
Murdock Vs Jules-X
Murdock Vs Wontime
Murray Richardson
Murvin Jay
Murvin Jay &
  Mr Suave
Mushroom
Muts
Mystic Waves
Mystik
Mystique
Mystique & Davidov
Mystique & Mad-D
Märtino Brös

N

N8N
Nabil
Namalee
Namissy
Namissy (Silk) & Kay
Nanasi & Vice
Natarcia
Nathan & Wax'X
Nathan Coles
Nathan Fake
Nathanael
Natural Born Deejays
Navid Tahernia
Neil
Neil Landstrumm
Nelson Rosado
Neon
Neophyte
Neven
Nic & Sa Femme
Nic'O Vegas
Nick
Nick Holder
Niclas
Nico
Nico Lombardi
Nico Purman
Nico Vegas
Nicola Conte
Nicolai
Nicolas Clays
Nicolaz
Nicolaï & Prinz
Nikolaï
Nikos Akrivos
Nils Hess
Nils Holgerffun
Nils Holgerffun &
  Ricky La Fête
Nid & Sancy
Niyi
Noise P
Noisecontrollers
Noizz
Nondejul
NongdeDJul
Norion
Norma Jean Bell
Norman Bates
Nu:Tone
Nubian
Nudex
Nymfo
Nymfo & Dmc

O

Obi-One
Odo 7
Okinawa 69

Ole Sollied
Oliver
Olivier Abbeloos
Olivier Gosseries
Olivier Pieters
Olivier Tjon
Olivier Vs Mario
One87 & Dmc
Onionz
Onur Özer
Opiate
Optical
Optimo
Organic Audio
Original Red
  Alert Sound
Orlando Voorn
Oscar Mulero
Osunlade
Oxia

P

Padded Cell
Pako & Frederik
Pan-Pot
Pantha Du Prince
Para One
Partyharders Squad
Pascal
Pascal F.E.O.S.
Pat
Pat Krimson
Patrick Pulsinger
Patrick Schmidt
Patrick Schmidt
  Vs Bartholomeo
Paul
Paul Johnson
Paul Kalkebrenner
Paul Murphy
Paul Oakenfold
Paul Van Dyk
Paul Ward
Pavo
Peanut Butterwolf
Pedro Winter
Pepsi Colin
Percy X
Perry O'Neil
Perspect
Peshay
Peshay & Mc Moose
Petar Dundov
Pete Adarkwah
Pete Heller
Pete Herbert
Pete Tong
Peter
Peter Aerts
Peter Boonen

Peter Boonen Soul
  Movement
Peter Lesage
Peter Luts
Peter Novak
Peter Pan & Friends
Pharoahe Monch
Phat Phil Cooper
Pheal
Phi Phi
Phil The Thrill
Philharmonix
Philip
Philip Michael
  Andersson
Philip Morgan
Philippe
Phill Da Cunha
Phill Weeks
Philou
Phonique
Photek
Phunk-E
Phuture 303
Phynn Vs Fred Baker
Pierce
Piere
Pierre
Pierre Blaszczyk
Pierre Elitair
Pierre H.
Pierre Vs Deg
Pierre Vs T-Quest
Pieter
Pig & Dan
Pilooski
Pink Satellite
Pipco
Pippe
Pirrès
Plaboys Vs Roland V
Plaid
Plastic Soul
  Orchestra
Plastiks Soundsystem
Plastyc Buddha
Ployd
Polazoid
Pole
Pole Folder
Polyester
Popof
Pota303
Pr Soundsystem
Praful
Praga Khan
Praxyd
Pril
Prince
Prins Thomas
Print
Prinz
Prinz & Filliz

Prinz & Tweety
Probe
Problem Kids
Prohackx
Promo
Promo Vs. Lady Dana
Psar
Psychogene
Pudde
Pulpo Club
Purple Moon DJ Team
Push

Q

Q-Ic
Quiet Village
  Project
Quinten
Quinten & Biens

R

R-Deem
Ra-Soul
Rac
Radio Infinity
Radio Slave
Raffa
Raffael
Rafh
Rainer Truby
Ralph Lawson
Ramon Tapia
Randall & Mc Fats
Randome Bloke
Rank 1
Raoul
Raoul Belmans
Raoul Lambert
Raphael
Raphael & Michiel
Raphaël
Ravin
Raw Deal
Ray Keith
Ray Mang
Rdml & Mc Della
Re:Nald & Krewl
Recloose
Red D
Red D & Lady Linn
Red D & San Soda
Red D Vs Ya'Mo
Red Snapper
Redhead
Regi & Wout
Regis
Reiner Truby
Remko
Remy

Renald Vs. Teck
Renato Cohen
Renaud
Rennie Pilgrem
Repeat
Rewind
Rezza
Ricardo
Ricardo Villalobos
Richard Brown Aka
　Cherry Bomb
Richard Les Crees
Richard S. Aka
　Padded Cell
Richie Hawtin
Richie Hawtin /
　Plastikman
Ricky Montanari
Ricky Rivaro
Rim-K
Rino Cerrone
Rinôçérôse
Riton
Rizzi'N'Linx
Rn Ober
Rob 'n' Zoopsie
Rob Mello
Rob Rob
Robberd
Robert Armani
Robert Hood
Robert Leiner
Robert Monreo
Robin Porter
Rocco
Rodney Hunter
Rodriguez
Roellove
Roga Vs Zawdi Mc
Roger Orb
Roger Sanchez
Roland Appel
Rolando
Rom 1
Rom 1 & Mc Della
Roma
Romain
Romain Bno
Romanthony
Ronald Molendijk
Ronald V. Gelderen
Roni Size
Ronny
Roog
Rooty
Roussia
Rub 'n' Tug
Rub A Dub Sound
Ruba J.
Rudy Rocket
Rudy Victor Ackaert
Russ Gabriel &
　Robin Lurie

Russel Stanton
Ruthless
Régis

S

S'N'K
S-Venus
S.C. Steel
Sake
Sake & Cosmic
Salvatore
Sam
Samseville
Samuel Jay
Samuel L Session
Sander Kleinenberg
Sandra
Sascha Funke
Sasha
Sasha & John Digweed
Saskia
Satanas
Savanah Station
Scan X
Schatrax
Scope DJ
Scot Project
Scott Bradford
Scott Grooves
Scratch Massive
Sean
Seb
Seba Lecompte
Sebastian
Sebastien Krieg
Sebeing
Sebinson
Sebo K
Secret Cinema
Selektor
Semtec
Sen Jan
Sense
Sentrik
Seppe
Serge
Serge Santiago
Sergey Sapunov
Serom
Serom & Asfalte
Sexmachines
Señor Funk
Shadow Dancer
Shakedown
Shameboy
Shapeshift.er
Sharam Jey
Sharp
Shermanology
Shimakum
Shinedoe

Shlomi Aber
Shonky
Shorty & Ricky D
Shovel
Showtek
Si Begg
Sigi
Sike'N'Easy
Silicon Scally
Silicone Soul
Simon Bassline Smith
　& Youngman Mc
Simon Dunmore
Simon Sez
Sims
Sin Palabras
SinDJin
Sir Ray
Sir Ray & El Niño
　Del Ritmo
Siskid
Sispeo
Skoere
Slam
Slo'Mo
Smith
Smith Davis
Smos & B.B.
Smos & Baby (B)
Smos & Baby B
Smos & Baby B.
Smos & Baby Bee
Smos & Baby N
Smos & Baby-B
Smos & Baby-Bee
Smos & Baby.B
Smos & Bb
Smos And Baby B
Smos And Baby B.
Smos And Baby Bee
Smos And Bb
Smos Baby Bee
Smos En Baby B
Smos N Baby Bee
Smoss & Baby B.
Snap!
Snof
Societe Anonyme
Solomun
Sonic Tonic
Sonik
Soul Designer
Soul Migrantz
Soul Phonic
Soul Preacher
Soultronik
Soulwax
Sound Of Stereo
Soundweapon Aka
　Fresh & Mc Ivory
Source Direct
Sovereign
　Roadshow 2000

Spacer
Spacid
Sparky Ninja
Spawniii
Special K
Speedy J
Spencer Parker
Spirit Catcher
Spiritcatcher
Squadra Bossa
   Feat. Buscemi
Squarepusher
St-Dic
St. Steel
Stacey Pullen
Stanny Franssen
   Aka G-Force
Stanny Franssen
   Vs Lowdown
Starfish Pool
Starflam
Starski & Tonic
Starski & Tweety
Steam
Steed
Steed & Zuri
Stef
Stefaan
Stefanie
Stefanie &
   Bobby Speed
Steff
Stephane
Stephane Vb
Stephanie
Stephanie Feat Wunmi
Stephanie Ft.
   Mc Philippo
Stephen
Steve
Steve & Phil
Steve Angello
Steve Bug
Steve Cop
Steve Pool
Steve Pool &
   Mystique
Steve Rachmad
Steve Stoll
Stijn
Stimming
Stl
Stol
Stone Warriors
Stuart Mc Lellan
Style Of Eye
Styrofoam
Stéphanie
Sugar Cain
Sugar Cain &
   Anthony More
Sultanz Of Zzwing
Sumsonic

Sun
Sunnery James &
   Ryan Marciano
Super Discount
Superpitcher
Surfing Leons
Surgeon
Surprise
   Superstart DJ
Sven & Aldo
Sven & Niclas
Sven Lanvin
Sven Van Hees
Sven Väth
Svenn
Swag
Swag All Night
   Soundsystem Feat
   Mark Bell
Sweatshop
Sweet Coffee
Sweet Coffee Light
Swirl People
Sylvain
System-D

T

T Hof Van Commerce
T-Quest
T. Carpenter &
   Billoved
T99 Aka Olivier
   Abbeloos
Takkyu Ishino
Tall M Klein
Tamurai
Tania Vulcano
Tatanka
TC Brain
Technasia
Technoboy
Technova
Tedd Patterson
Teebee
Teenage Bad Girl
Tek 9
Telepopmusic
Temmesta
Tempted Audio
Terence Fixmer
Terry Francis
Terry Francis Vs
   Nathan Coles
Terry Hunter
Terry Toner
Thang
The Advent
The Advent Live
The Avalanches
The Backlash
The Bays

The Beholder Vs
   The Prophet
The Bloody Honkies
The Chef Ft.
   Mc Red 1
The Dark Raver
The Dominators
   (Jan Van Biesen
   Vs T-Quest)
The Electric
   Miles Project
The Freestyle
   Institute
The Glimmer Twins
The Glimmers
The Hacker
The Heavies
The Jelly Bellies
The Jokari Club
The Juan Maclean
The Lotterboys
The Love Brothers
The Milkshakerz
The Milkshakerz
   Vs Ac/DJ
The Neon Judgement
The Nitrous
The Oyl Butchers
The Poodle Himself
The Prophet
The Rudy'S
The Scientists
The Subs
The Turntable
   Dubbers
The Viper
The Youngsters
Theo Parrish
Thierry Princiotta
Thierry Steady Go
Thierry Tallier
Thimbles
Thomas Andersson
Thomas Brinkmann
Thomas Krome
Thomas Little
Thomas Muller
Thomaz
Thompzz
Thrillseekers
Tibo'Z
Tiefschwarz
Tiga
Tiger Stripes
Tigra
Tim
Tim 'Love' Lee
Tim Deluxe
Tim Paris
Tim Sweeney
Tim Vs Psychogene
Timaxx
Timo Maas

Timothé
Tina
Tinez
Tino
Tino & Raoul
Tipper
Tipsy & Thelma
Tiresz
Titlight
Tito & Echo Virus
Tiësto
Tlp
Tlp & Dors
Tlp Aka Troubleman
Tlp Vs Davidov
Tm & Vista
Toaster Soulmc
Tobias Schmidt
Tobias Thomas
Toby
Todd Terje
Todd Terry
Tofke
Toka Project
Tokta
Tom & Dickie
Tom Baker
Tom Barman
Tom De Neef
Tom Leclerq
Tom Middleton
Tom Parris
Tomas
Tomaz
Tommy
Toni Rios
Tony
Tony Humphries
Tony Thomas
Total Science
Tox
Tractor
Trailerkids
Trakse
Trentemoller
Treva Whateva
Triple R
Tripoli
Trish
Trish & Kash
Trish van Eynde
Trix & Dollars
Trixie
Trouble Fun
Troubleman
Troubleman Aka Tlp
Troubleman Nr. 1
Troy Pierce
Tummy Touch DJ'S
Turntable Dubbers
Tuttu Matto
Tweety

Tweety & Bartholomeo
Twinz
Twinz Aka Mad-D
  & Vista
Tyrant

U

U-Gene & Oh-Jay
U-Ziq
Ugo
Ultrasonic
Umek
Underwolves
Uneak & Crack T.
Unit Moebius
Upperclass Junkies

V

Vann & Path
Vanno
Vark Vee
Vasithy
Versus
Vertigo
Vice
Vince
Vince Hilton
Vista
Vitali Kornev
Vitalic
Vive La Fête
Volta
Vorax
Vortex & Brekbit

W

Waldo
Wally Lopez
Walter
Wappe & Wikke
Wax Doctor
Whizz
Who Made Who
Wighnomy Brothers
Wighnomy Brothers
  Ft. Robach Wruhme
Will O'Brien
William Hunt
Wim Sallinger
Wine Guns
Winston Hazel
Wontime
Wontime & Ricky D
Wontime & System-D
Woodcarver
Working Class Hero

X

X-Ian
X-Press 2
X-Tian
X-Ven Xanadu
Xentrix
Xentrix & Jlk

Y

Ya'Mo
Ya'Mo & His Live
  Elements
Ya'Mo Vs Red D
  Feat. Lady Linn
Yahel
Yan
Yannick
Yen Sung
Yoji Biomehanika
Yoshi Tsuko &
  Csystem
Youri
Yvan Smagghe
Yves
Yves 'E' Zone
Yves Croky
Yves Deruyter
Yves V
Yves-E-Zone

Z

Zander Vt
Zany
Zatox
Zohm
Zolex
Zzino

#

100% Isis
100% Vooraan
16 Bit Lolittas
187
1982 Motor
2000 And One
2000 Watt
2Nd Gen
2Winz
4 Hero
4Hero
4K'N'Temper
50 Foot Combo

DJ INDEX

COLOPHON

Written by Koen Galle (editor in chief)

Flyers photographed by Baby Bee
from her and Smos' archive

Photography by Benoit Meeus, Jockum Klenell,
Baby Bee & Jamila De Backer

Cover image: Baby Bee
Image page 3: Jamila De Backer

Designed by Otis Verhoeve, set in *Syncro* (Out of the Dark)

Testimonials from Jamila De Backer, Pierre Noisiez, Dirk Deruyck,
Steve Cop, Dave Brody, Raoul Belmans, Philip De Liser, Brandy Volant,
Jane Haesen, Ward Van Den Bogerd, Geert Sermon, Colin McBean,
Jan Van Biesen, Filip van Moerkercke, Julien Veniel, Frie Verhelst,
Stéphanie D'Olieslager, Patrick Soks, Floris Machiels, Jan Machiels,
Bart Van Neste, Jacques Garotta, Koen van Immerseel & Benoit Meeus

Thanks to Pieter Vochten, Yves Kerremans, Frédéric Leemans,
Nina Serulus & Elias Derboven.

Printed by die Keure
on *Forever Citron Yellow* 120 g/m² and *Magno Gloss* 115 g/m²

Edition of 1000

ISBN
9789464780406

Published by

AfterClub Publishing

2023